Active Assessment

FOR THE
NATIONAL CURRICULUM

by

Sandra Dinsdale and Anne Tracey

SCHOFIELD AND SIMS LTD   HUDDERSFIELD

© 1991 SCHOFIELD & SIMS LTD

0 7217 3044 2

First printed 1991

All rights reserved. No reproduction, copy or transmission of this publication may be made without written permission, except under the terms set out below.

This publication is copyright. After purchase, teachers are free to reproduce any part of **Active Assemblies for the National Curriculum** provided that the copies are for use in Class or School Assemblies in the educational establishment of purchase only. For copying under any other circumstances prior permission must be obtained from the publishers and a fee may be payable.
Public Performances of any part of this work are not allowed.

Any person who does any unauthorised act in relation to this publication will be liable to criminal prosecution and civil claims for damages.

Typesetting by Armitage Typo/Graphics Ltd, Huddersfield
Printed in Great Britain by The Amadeus Press Ltd, Huddersfield

Contents

Attainment Targets	4
Key to Hymn and Song Books	6
Preface	6
Suggestions as to how to use this book	7
Ourselves	9
Friends and Neighbours	17
Harvest	23
War and Peace	30
Energy	36
Communications	42
A King is Born	48
China	54
Light	60
Amazing Grace	66
Mother's Day	72
Time	78
The Earth in Space	84
New Beginnings	90
All Creatures Great and Small	96
Conservation – An Assembly for May Day	102
The Other Man's Grass is Always Greener	108
Sport for All	114
Sound	120
Music	127

Attainment Targets

OURSELVES

SCIENCE:	AT3	Processes of Life: Levels 1, 2b, 3a, 4a, 4b, 5c, 5e.
ENGLISH:	AT1	Speaking and Listening: Levels 1, 2a, 2d, 2e, 4, 5d, 6b, 6c.
	AT2	Reading: Levels 3a, 4a.

FRIENDS AND NEIGHBOURS

ENGLISH:	AT1	Speaking and Listening: Levels 1, 2a, 2d, 2e, 4, 5d, 6b, 6c.
	AT2	Reading: Levels 3a, 4a.
	AT3	Writing: Levels 2a, 2b, 3a, 3b, 3d, 3e, 4a, 4c, 4d, 4e, 5a, 5b, 5d, 5e, 6a, 6b, 6c, 6d.

HARVEST

ENGLISH:	AT1	Speaking and Listening: Levels 1, 2a, 2d, 2e, 4, 5d, 6b, 6c.
	AT2	Reading: Levels 3a, 4a

WAR AND PEACE

ENGLISH:	AT1	Speaking and Listening: Levels 1, 2a, 2d, 2e, 4, 5d, 6b, 6c.
	AT2	Reading: Levels 3a, 4a.
	AT3	Writing: Levels 2, 3, 4, 5, 6.

ENERGY

SCIENCE:	AT13	Energy: Levels 4b, 4c, 5, 6a, 6d, 7c.
ENGLISH:	AT1	Speaking and Listening: Levels 1, 2a, 2d, 2e, 4, 5d, 6b, 6c.
	AT2	Reading: Levels 3a, 4a.

COMMUNICATIONS

SCIENCE:	AT12	The scientific aspects of information technology including microelectronics: Levels 1, 2a, 2b, 3b, 4a.
ENGLISH:	AT1	Speaking and Listening: Levels 1, 2a, 2d, 2e, 4, 5d, 6b, 6c.
	AT2	Reading: Levels 3a, 4a.

A KING IS BORN

ENGLISH:	AT1	Speaking and Listening: Levels 1, 2a, 2d, 2e, 4, 5d, 6b, 6c.
	AT2	Reading: Levels 3a, 4a.
	AT3	Writing: Levels 2a, 3a, 3b, 3d, 3e, 4a, 4c, 4d, 4e, 5b, 5d.

CHINA

ENGLISH:	AT1	Speaking and Listening: Levels 1, 2a, 2d, 2e, 4, 5d, 6b, 6c.
	AT2	Reading: Levels 3a, 4a.
TECHNOLOGY:	AT1	Identifying needs and opportunities: Levels 2c, 3b, 4a, 4f, 5a, 6a
	AT2	Generating a design: Levels 1, 2a, 3, 4, 5a, 5b, 5c, 5d, 6a, 6c.
	AT3	Planning and making: Levels 2a, 2b, 2c, 3, 4b, 4c, 4d, 4e, 5.
	AT4	Evaluating: Levels 2a, 3a, 3b, 4a, 4b, 5a, 5b.

LIGHT

SCIENCE:	AT15	Using light and electromagnetic radiation: Levels 1, 3a, 4, 5.
ENGLISH:	AT1	Speaking and Listening: Levels 1, 2a, 2d, 2e, 4, 5d, 6b, 6c.
	AT2	Reading: Levels 3a, 4a.

AMAZING GRACE

ENGLISH:	AT1	Speaking and Listening: Levels 1, 2a, 2d, 2e, 4, 5d, 6b, 6c.
	AT2	Reading: Levels 3a, 4a.

MOTHER'S DAY

ENGLISH:	AT1	Speaking and Listening: Levels 1, 2, 4d, 5d, 6c.
	AT2	Reading: Levels 3a, 4a.

Attainment Targets

TIME

SCIENCE:	AT16	The Earth in Space: Levels 3b, 4a.
MATHEMATICS:	AT8	Measures: Levels 2c, 3b
ENGLISH:	AT1	Speaking and Listening: Levels 1, 2a, 2d, 2e, 4, 5d, 6b, 6c.
	AT2	Reading: Levels 3a, 4a

THE EARTH IN SPACE

SCIENCE:	AT16	The Earth in Space: Levels 1b, 2, 4, 5a, 6.
ENGLISH:	AT1	Speaking and Listening: Levels 1, 2a, 2d, 2e, 4, 5d, 6b, 6c.
	AT2	Reading: Levels 3a, 4a.
TECHNOLOGY:	AT1	Identifying needs: Levels 2c, 3b, 4a, 5a, 6c.
	AT2	Generating a design: Levels 1, 2a, 3, 4, 5a, 5b, 5c, 5d, 6a, 6c.
	AT3	Planning and making: Levels 2a, 2b, 2c, 3, 4b, 4c, 4d, 4e, 5.
	AT4	Evaluating: Levels 2a, 3a, 3b, 4a, 4b, 5a, 5b.

NEW BEGINNINGS

ENGLISH:	AT1	Speaking and Listening: Levels 1, 2a, 2d, 2e, 4, 5d, 6b, 6c.
	AT2	Reading: Levels 3a, 4a.
	AT3	Writing: Levels 2a, 2b, 3a, 3b, 3d, 3e, 4a, 4c, 4d, 4e, 5a, 5b, 5d, 5e, 6a, 6b, 6c, 6d.
TECHNOLOGY:	AT1	Identifying needs and opportunities: Levels 2c, 3b.
	AT2	Generating a design: Levels 1, 2a, 3, 4, 5, 6a, 6c.
	AT3	Planning and making: Levels 1, 2, 3, 4, 5, 6a, 6b, 6d, 6e.
	AT4	Evaluating: Levels 1a, 2a, 3b, 4a, 4b, 5a, 5b, 6a, 6c.

ALL CREATURES GREAT AND SMALL

SCIENCE:	AT2	The variety of life: Levels 1, 2a, 2b, 3b, 5d.
ENGLISH:	AT1	Speaking and Listening: Levels 1, 2a, 2d, 2e, 4, 5d, 6b, 6c.
	AT2	Reading: Levels 3a, 4a.

CONSERVATION – AN ASSEMBLY FOR MAY DAY

SCIENCE:	AT5	Human influences on the Earth: Levels 1, 3a, 5a, 6c.
ENGLISH:	AT1	Speaking and Listening: Levels 1, 2a, 2d, 2e, 4, 5d, 6b, 6c.
	AT2	Reading: Levels 3a, 4a.

THE OTHER MAN'S GRASS IS ALWAYS GREENER

ENGLISH:	AT1	Speaking and Listening: Levels 1, 2a, 2d, 2e, 4, 5d, 6b, 6c.
	AT2	Reading: Levels 3a, 4a.

SPORT FOR ALL

ENGLISH:	AT1	Speaking and Listening: Levels 1, 2a, 2d, 2e, 4, 5d, 6b, 6c.
	AT2	Reading: Levels 3a, 4a.

SOUND

SCIENCE:	AT14	Sound and Music: Levels 1, 2a, 3, 4, 5, 6a, 6b.
ENGLISH:	AT1	Speaking and Listening: Levels 1, 2a, 2d, 2e, 4, 5d, 6b, 6c.
	AT2	Reading: Levels 3a, 4a.
TECHNOLOGY:	AT1	Identifying needs and opportunities: Levels 2c, 3b, 4a, 5a, 6c.
	AT2	Generating a design: Levels 1, 2a, 3, 4, 5a, 5b, 5c, 5d, 6a, 6c.
	AT3	Planning and making: Levels 2a, 2b, 2c, 3, 4b, 4c, 4d, 4e, 5.
	AT4	Evaluating: Levels 2a, 3a, 3b, 4a, 4b, 5a, 5b.

MUSIC

SCIENCE:	AT14	Sound and Music: Levels 1, 2b, 3a, 5a.
ENGLISH:	AT1	Speaking and Listening: Levels 1, 2a, 2d, 2e, 4, 5d, 6b, 6c.
	AT2	Reading: Levels 3a, 4a.
TECHNOLOGY:	AT1	Identifying needs and opportunities: Levels 2c, 3b, 4a, 5a, 6c.
	AT2	Generating a design: Levels 1, 2a, 3, 4, 5a, 5b, 5c, 5d, 6a, 6c.
	AT3	Planning and making: Levels 2a, 2b, 2c, 3, 4b, 4c, 4d, 4e, 5.
	AT4	Evaluating: Levels 2a, 3a, 3b, 4a, 4b, 5a, 5b.

Preface

This book consists of twenty child-centred, National Curriculum-based assemblies with a strong emphasis on pupil participation in an enjoyable active learning situation. In its radical approach to methodology, it brings together the cross-curricular themes of Religious Studies, English, Science, Technology, Mathematics, Music and Drama. In presenting an assembly, which is best done on a class or year group basis, the children will be able to draw on and develop their knowledge and skills in a variety of subjects and use a combination of communication techniques.

The assemblies are suitable for use in Junior, Middle or Lower Secondary Schools. Some are written with younger children in mind and some may be more suitable for older children but all can be adapted to suit any age group. Each assembly can be used in its entirety or in part. The National Curriculum requires children to study many of the topics we have chosen. A list of National Curriculum attainment targets precedes this Preface and each assembly. The level of achievement reached will depend on the ability and maturity of the children.

Although the assemblies are of a broadly Christian character, their moral, religious and social messages have been created bearing in mind the developing needs of a multi-cultural and multi-racial society. It is hoped the assemblies will help to promote an understanding of the needs and beliefs of other people and cultures, now and in the past.

The children will learn to interact with one another and will enjoy sharing their experiences with a wide range of audiences. This book is a novel and innovative way of helping children to explore and understand many National Curriculum targets. ACTIVE ASSEMBLIES FOR THE NATIONAL CURRICULUM is an invaluable aid for the busy teacher who wants to deliver the National Curriculum in an original, enjoyable and entertaining way.

Key to Hymn and Song Books

REFERRED TO THROUGHOUT *ACTIVE ASSEMBLIES FOR THE NATIONAL CURRICULUM*

A	Alleluya, A & C Black
AP	Apusskidu, A & C Black
CAP	Come and Praise, B.B.C.
CC	Christmas Carols, Sphere
CGC	Carol Gaily Carol, A & C Black
GBSB	Great British Song Book, Pavilion
JH	The Jolly Herring, A & C Black
LGBH	The Little Golden Book of Hymns, F. Muller
MHB	Morning Has Broken, Schofield & Sims
NSC	New Songs for Children, Wise
RMHOL	Russian Melodies, Hymns of Other Lands
SOP	Songs of Praise, Oxford University Press
SSS	Sacred Songs and Solos, Marshall, Morgan & Scott
ST	Sing True, Religious Educational Press
TA	Ta-ra-ra boom-de-ay, A & C Black
TTS	A Time to Sing, Macmillan Education
WCV	With Cheerful Voice, A & C Black

Suggestions as to how to use this book

TEXT

One of the main aims of this book is to present complete scripts for assemblies. To facilitate this, the book can be photocopied so that each child can have his or her own copy of the assembly. The layout is such that the pages can be folded and made into an easily manageable booklet. In each script, space has been left after the headings, "Narrator" etc. so that children's names can be inserted. Stage instructions are interspersed in bold type throughout the text.
If each child can have a copy of the script it will enable them to become more involved during preparation and rehearsals.

CHARACTERS

When selecting the characters for an assembly, certain children will obviously be more suitable for particular roles. This may depend on ability, size, appearance and/or personality. As many children as possible should participate. The authors suggest that a different child is used for each 'Narrator' part. The authors have found that auditioning for the major speaking parts assists the selection process.

ORGANISATION

Where a stage or blocks are available, all the children involved in the assembly can be seated at floor level, facing the audience. Where a stage is not available, the audience can be seated in a semi-circular arrangement. The children involved in the assembly can be seated completing the circle. The performance can take place in the centre. It will only be necessary for characters to leave their seats when they are about to perform. They can return to their places at an appropriate time, such as during a scene change or applause.

PROPS

The use of costume and props where available would greatly enhance the performance of all the assemblies. The children may be able to provide most of these. Where teachers wish to make props, cardboard boxes can be transformed into virtually anything. In the assemblies where technology targets are stated, certain props could be the subject of a technology project depending on the time and materials available. These are listed below:

CHINA	– Kites and a Chinese dragon
THE EARTH IN SPACE	– Spaceship
NEW BEGINNINGS	– Easter bonnets
SOUND	– Decibel detector
MUSIC	– Musical instruments

However, even these props can be very speedily and simply constructed. For example, a Chinese dragon can be made from decorated cardboard boxes, a spaceship can be quite adequately represented by a stage block covered in silver foil and a decibel detector can readily be made from a decorated cardboard box with a set of headphones attached.

MUSIC

The musical items cited in this book are suggestions only and can be replaced by others on a similar theme. The suggested hymns and songs are to be found in a variety of hymnals and song books, though only one source will be given in the text. This will be in the form of an abbreviation. The full titles are given on page 6. Other musical items are readily available on record or cassette. These could be obtained from the music section of a local library or from the children in school. When performing songs, the children can sing to the record or cassette or be accompanied. The instruction 'All sing' refers to all the children involved in the assembly.

Acknowledgements

The authors and the publishers wish to thank the following for permission to use copyright material:

Cassell PLC, for **Thoughts From a Kitchen** by Mary Ormsby, from *The Senior Teachers Assembly Book* by D M Prescott

Gill and Macmillan Ltd., for **The Telephone** by Michel Quoist, from *Prayers of Life*

Hutchinson Publishing Group, for an extract from *The You-Two* by Jean Ure

John Murray (Publishers) Ltd., for an extract from **1940** and an extract from **Advent 1955** by John Betjeman from *Uncollected Poems*

Margaret Ramsey Ltd., for an extract from **The Well-Off Kid** by Bill Naughton from *The Goalkeeper's Revenge*

Stanley Thornes (Publishers) Ltd., for an extract from **An Earwig in the Ear** by Nigel Gray

Every effort has been made to trace the owners of all work included in this Assembly Book. Should any work have been included for which the copyright is still in existence, but for which no acknowledgement has been made, we express our regret. If any such cases are drawn to our notice we shall be pleased to make due acknowledgement and correct this in future editions.

Ourselves PAGE 1

ATTAINMENT TARGETS
SCIENCE: AT3 Processes of life: Levels 1, 2b, 3a, 4a, 4b, 5c, 5e.
ENGLISH: AT1 Speaking and Listening: Levels 1, 2a, 2d, 2e, 4, 5d, 6b, 6c.
AT2 Reading: Levels 3a, 4a.

CHARACTERS

Up to 9 Narrators	Cave-dwellers	Protein
Mr. Stone	Bod E	Vitamin
Mrs. Stone	6 children to describe	Carbohydrate
Loni	organs of the body	Lollipop Lil
Wolf	Doctor	Chorus
Lion	Patient	Prayer Leader

NARRATOR

There are millions of living things in the world, plants, animals, insects and other creatures. Human beings are just one of the many kinds of life on earth. Humans are the most advanced animal so far. For better or for worse we rule over other living things on earth.

NARRATOR

When I look up at the heavens,
At the wonderful work of God's hand,
The moon and the stars that He fashioned,
I think I can just understand
That man is a little below the angels,
And God has set him to be
In charge of the birds and creatures,
And the fish that live in the sea.

(From Psalm 8)

Ourselves PAGE 2

Suggested Hymn: "HE MADE ME" (TTS)

NARRATOR

One of the main differences between humans and other animals is the brain. The human brain is much more highly developed than the brains of other animals. Our larger, more intelligent brain thinks up ideas. Our skilful hands carry out those ideas. Our body's bone structure, muscles and upright posture help make it possible to carry out the most difficult tasks. All living things have changed very slowly over millions of years. The human brain slowly developed as intelligence became important in order to track food and escape from enemies. People today are very different in many ways from their ancestors of many thousands of years ago.
Early men and women lived in caves and had to hunt for their food in order to survive.

Enter Mr and Mrs Stone and daughter Loni

MR STONE

(To wife) I'm off hunting. Are you coming?

MRS STONE

I've got to fetch the water so you'll have to take our Loni with you.

Ourselves — PAGE 3

MR STONE

She's not coming with me, she's useless. Last time I took her hunting, we were all ready for the big kill when she sneezed and the reindeer got away.

MRS STONE

Well she's not coming with me to the river because the last time she came she fell in. She'll have to stay here on her own.

LONI

Oh don't leave me in this big dark cave by myself.

MR STONE

You'll be all right girl. Got to grow up sometime.

Mr and Mrs Stone exit

LONI

Oh it's scary in here by myself. **(Warily explores cave)** I know, I'll make a trap in case a wild animal comes along. How else can I protect myself? **(Kneels)** First I'll dig a pit as deep as I can using Dad's flint axe and scraper. **(Digs a pit but becoming increasingly tired)** Now I need to cover it with branches and leaves.

Ourselves — PAGE 4

(Collects twigs and branches from side stage and carefully lays them over imaginary hole) Now the finishing touches, a piece of reindeer meat to tempt him. **(Brings a piece of reindeer meat and lays it on top of the pit)** I'm worn out after such hard work, I'll have to have a rest. **(Goes to back of cave and lies down)**

Enter Wolf who prowls round cave, sees reindeer meat, goes to eat, falls in trap and hurts paw

WOLF

(Crying with pain) Oh my paw, my paw it hurts, it hurts! I can't stand the pain!

Loni emerges from the back of the cave, nervously approaches the trap, looks inside, jumps back and screams

LONI

It's a wolf, a vicious wolf!

WOLF

Help me, please help me!

LONI

Not a chance! You'll eat me all up.

Ourselves — PAGE 5

WOLF
No I won't, indeed, indeed I won't. Cub's honour.

LONI
Are you a wolf cub?

WOLF
Sure I am. I am a........................
(**Name of local cub group can be inserted here**)

LONI
That's all right then. Out you come. (**Pulls him out. Wolf cries in pain**)

LONI
Let's have a look at that paw. I'll try some of mum's herbal remedy. (**Rubs remedy on paw**)

WOLF
Oh that feels good!

Enter lion roaring. Loni screams. Wolf fights lion and wins. Lion lies dead on floor. Enter Mr and Mrs Stone

Ourselves — PAGE 6

MR STONE
What on earth have you been up to, our Loni?

MRS STONE
(**Screams**) A lion and a wolf.

LONI
It's all right, the wolf is my friend. He saved me from this terrible lion. Can he stay and live with us in our cave?

MR STONE
What, have a wolf as a pet?

LONI
Well he did save my life.

MR STONE
What do you think Wilma?

MRS STONE
Oh she'll complain for weeks if you say no. Let him stay.

Ourselves — PAGE 7

MR STONE

Come on, let's get this lion skinned. We'll invite some friends to share our feast. **(All exit dragging lion with them)**

Enter cave-dwellers. All dance to "CAVEMAN ROCK" as sung by Tommy Steele

NARRATOR

Although the way we live now is very different to that of Early Man, the functions of the body are still the same. To live, you have to breathe, eat and drink, move and know what is happening around you. Your body must be able to get rid of wastes, protect itself against disease and repair itself. All the functions of the body affect each other and are controlled by the brain.

NARRATOR

We will now look more closely at one particular human called Bod E.

A child enters as Bod E

The following section has been written by children as a result of their own research and is given as an example. Children may write and read their own research

Ourselves — PAGE 8

NARRATOR

The brain.

1ST CHILD

(Points to the position of the brain on Bod E)
The most exciting things in the world happen inside your head. This is where your brain is. The brain is the part of the body which tells it how to work. It tells your stomach to begin to digest your food, it tells your heart to beat like a drum, it even tells you how to move and how to stand still. Even when you are in a deep sleep, your brain still keeps on working as you dream.

NARRATOR

The heart.

2ND CHILD

(Points to the position of the heart on Bod E)
The heart is a kind of pump which drives blood around the body. Valves in the heart stop the blood from flowing backwards. Your heart is about the size of your fist and has four parts or chambers.

Ourselves — PAGE 9

NARRATOR

The lungs.

3RD CHILD

(Points to the position of the lungs on Bod E)
The lungs receive the air you breathe through your nose and mouth. Air contains the oxygen that is eventually needed to convert food into energy.
The lungs are made of hundreds of thousands of balloon-like air sacs and are protected by the rib cage.

NARRATOR

The stomach.

4TH CHILD

(Points to the position of the stomach on Bod E)
The stomach is like a soft bag with an opening at each end, squeezing and moving all the time. The food stays for a while in the stomach and is then moved on to the intestine. All this time it is being mixed with different juices to dissolve the food. It is then taken through the sides of the intestine where it is dissolved in the blood.

Ourselves — PAGE 10

NARRATOR

The liver.

5TH CHILD

(Points to the position of the liver on Bod E)
The liver is the largest organ in your body. The blood containing the digested food goes first to the liver. The liver purifies the blood and stores sugars and fats until the body needs them.

NARRATOR

The kidneys.

6TH CHILD

(Points to the position of the kidneys on Bod E)
We have two kidneys. They are bean shaped and about 10 centimetres long. All the blood has to run through the kidneys. The kidneys make urine and they filter out harmful wastes made by the body.

Ourselves — PAGE 11

NARRATOR

The body is one unit even though it is made up of many different parts. St. Paul, in his letter to the Corinthians, says that, the people in the Christian religion are also one body or unit even though every individual member has different gifts and personality. What a ridiculous situation it would be if the eye argued that it was more important than the ear. The eye and the ear are both different but both very important parts of the body. Sometimes people say "I could never do what you do" and they get discouraged. We should not measure our own abilities against others because we each have our own unique job to do.

Children sing

"I GOT LIFE" from "Hair"

NARRATOR

When one part of the body fails to function, then the whole body suffers. If a bad tooth begins to ache, even though the tooth is only a very small part of the body, it can cause a great deal of suffering. If the heart stops beating, the body is starved of oxygen and quickly dies. Doctors can sometimes massage a heart which has stopped and start it beating again.

Enter DOCTOR and PATIENT and mime actions and words of the song "OH DOCTOR I'M IN TROUBLE" as sung by Sophia Loren and Peter Sellers.

Ourselves — PAGE 12

NARRATOR

Given a chance, the body can look after itself. However, the way we live can make it hard for the body to keep itself working properly. To keep our bodies healthy we must eat a balanced diet.
A "balanced" diet means a good mixture of foods that contain proteins, vitamins, carbohydrates, fats, minerals, fibre and water.

Enter Protein, Vitamin and Carbohydrate

PROTEIN

I am a protein and I am a body-building food. I come from animals and some plants. You will find me in meat, fish, eggs and milk and also in peas, beans and nuts.

VITAMIN

I am a vitamin and I am extremely important for keeping you healthy. You will find some of me in most foods but mostly in raw or lightly-cooked fruit and vegetables.

CARBOHYDRATE

I am a carbohydrate and I am an energy-giving food. I come mainly from plants and I contain plenty of starch or sugar. You will find me in bread, potatoes, rice and sweet foods. My sugar is useful only for instant energy. It does not help you to grow except to grow fat and can ruin your teeth. Oh no! Here comes Lollipop Lil. She's got a real craving for my sugar. I'm off.

**Exit Carbohydrate, followed by Vitamin and Protein.
Enter Lollipop Lil with a giant lollipop and sings or mimes to
"ON THE GOOD SHIP LOLLIPOP" as sung by Shirley Temple**

**At the end of the music Lollipop Lil falls asleep
Enter Carbohydrate**

CARBOHYDRATE

Is it safe to come in? The only time she stops looking for me is when she is asleep. Mind you, even then she's dreaming about me. Sweet dreams, Lollipop. I expect she'll wake up with tummy ache but it's only a matter of time before she's got toothache as well as tummy ache. She's gone to bed again without cleaning her teeth. There'll be a horrid, sticky, colourless layer called plaque forming on them. The sugar from all those sweets she's been eating will join up with the bacteria in the plaque to make a tooth-decaying acid.

Lollipop Lil wakes up. She jumps out of bed and runs around with her lollipop, crying

LOLLIPOP LIL

Tooth-decaying acid! Help! Help!   **(To the audience)** Can anyone help?   **(Freezes)**

Enter Narrator

NARRATOR

(To the audience)   The only one who can help Lollipop Lil is herself. She must avoid eating so many sweets, which cause plaque and decay. Good crunchy foods, like raw carrots, would be good for her and good for her teeth and gums. It is very important that she brushes her teeth and visits the dentist regularly.

CARBOHYDRATE

Come on Lollipop! There's no time to lose. I'll have that and you have this.   **(Takes Lollipop's lollipop and gives her a toothbrush)**   You've got a lot to learn.

All exit

Ourselves   PAGE 15

NARRATOR

It is only by getting to know all about ourselves that we can appreciate how fascinating the human body is and understand how to look after it.

PRAYER

We thank You God for our understanding of the past, for the stories and the facts.
We thank You for ourselves, body, mind and spirit. Help us to make the most of ourselves by taking care of our bodies and learning to use them to the best of our ability, not just for ourselves but for those we are with, day by day.

AMEN

Children sing

"GETTING TO KNOW YOU" from "The King and I"

Notes

Friends and Neighbours

PAGES 1&2

ATTAINMENT TARGETS
ENGLISH: AT1   Speaking and listening: Levels 1, 2a, 2d, 2e, 4, 5d, 6b, 6c.
          AT2   Reading: Levels 3a, 4a.
          AT3   Writing: Levels 2a, 2b, 3a, 3b, 3d, 3e, 4a, 4c, 4d, 4e, 5a, 5b, 5d, 5e, 6a, 6b, 6c, 6d.

CHARACTERS

Up to 11 Narrators
12 Dancers
Elizabeth Muir – (dark, straight hair)
Paddy Dewar – (not curly hair)
Children to read prose/poetry
2 children to sing "ANYTHING YOU CAN DO"

Chorus
1st Traveller
Priest
2nd Traveller
Samaritan

NARRATOR

One of the most important things we do is to choose other people to be our friends. People often choose friends who are similar to themselves in many ways, such as their age, background, interests and beliefs. There came a time when Jesus knew that he must choose a band of men who would be his faithful disciples, and carry on his work when he was no longer with them. It was very important that Jesus should choose the right men, so he spent a long time praying to God about his choice. With God's help he chose twelve men to help him to spread the word of God and to be his special friends. Their names were Simon, who Jesus called Peter; Andrew, his brother; James and John; Philip, Matthew, Bartholomew, Thomas, Thaddeus; another James, another Simon, and Judas Iscariot.

All sing and a group of children dance

"PUT YOUR HAND IN THE HAND" as sung by Joan Baez (A)

NARRATOR

Occasionally it is necessary to make new friends. This is sometimes difficult especially if you are completely new to the neighbourhood. Elizabeth Muir had to change school in the middle of the term because her family were moving house. Because her new school was so different from her old one, Elizabeth felt sure she'd never fit in. She was very unhappy at the end of her first morning. However, when she returned to school after lunch, Elizabeth met a girl called Paddy Dewar who became her special friend.

Enter Elizabeth with her schoolbag and stands alone in the playground for a while. Paddy enters and walks over to Elizabeth

PADDY

Hello.

ELIZABETH

Hello.   (The two girls stare at each other for a while)

PADDY

What's your name?

Friends and Neighbours

PAGES 3&4

ELIZABETH

Elizabeth Muir.

PADDY

I'm Paddy Dewar. Why have you started in the middle of a term?

ELIZABETH

We moved.

PADDY

Where from?

ELIZABETH

From Caterham.

PADDY

Are you glad you've come here? **(Elizabeth grunts)** Didn't you want to?

ELIZABETH

(Shrugs) Didn't mind.

PADDY

Don't you think you're going to like it?

ELIZABETH

Not sure.

PADDY

Did you like your old school? Was it better than this one?

ELIZABETH

It was different.

PADDY

Different how?

ELIZABETH

Well, it was – it was smaller.

PADDY

Was it posh? Did it have a uniform? What colour was it?

Friends and Neighbours

PAGES 5&6

ELIZABETH

Brown and gold.

PADDY

I bet you wish that you were still there. **(Elizabeth does not reply)** I s'pose someone's already asked you to be part of their gang? **(Elizabeth shakes her head)** Would you want to be if they did?

ELIZABETH

Don't know.

PADDY

You don't have to be. We could be a you-two, if you wanted.

ELIZABETH

What's a you-two?

PADDY

It's where two people are best friends and go around together and do things together and everyone says, "Hey, you two". It's better than being in a gang. Anyone can be in a gang. D'you want to?

ELIZABETH

(Smiles) All right.

PADDY

You have to show people. **(Paddy and Elizabeth link arms and march round the playground)**

BOTH

We're in a you-two, a you-two, a you-two... **(They stand still)**

PADDY

Did you have a best friend at your other school?

ELIZABETH

Yes.

PADDY

What was her name?

ELIZABETH

Jenny Bell.

Friends and Neighbours

PAGES 7&8

PADDY

Was she pretty?

ELIZABETH

I s'pose so.

PADDY

What colour hair did she have?

ELIZABETH

Fair.

PADDY

Fair like Julie's? People think she's pretty. I don't. I don't like fair hair. I like dark hair – dark and straight. Like yours. Was hers straight?

ELIZABETH

No. It was curly.

PADDY

I don't like curly hair. If I had curly hair I'd get it all cut off. Will you go on seeing her now that you're not at the same school?

ELIZABETH

I don't expect I will, not now.

PADDY

Anyway, she doesn't rhyme like we do... Elizabeth Muir and Paddy Dewar... Now that we're a you-two, shall I ask Jo Ann if she'll change places with me so we can sit together? We've got to do things together now that we're a you-two. There wouldn't be any point otherwise.

Extract from "THE YOU-TWO" by Jean Ure

All sing

"YOU'VE GOT A FRIEND" as sung by James Taylor

NARRATOR

The following rules of friendship came from a survey of what people wanted from their friends.
1. Keep secrets.
2. Share your happy times as well as your sad times.
3. Stand up for your friend.
4. Make sure you return borrowed things.
5. If your friend hurts your feelings, say so. Do not go off in a sulk.
6. Offer help; do not wait for your friend to ask.

The children can read some of their own work on what they think makes a good friend. This can be in poetry or prose

Friends and Neighbours

PAGES 9&10

NARRATOR

Friendship involves a great deal of give and take. Sometimes however, friends become jealous of each other and even the best of friends have disagreements and end up "falling out". They sometimes call each other names or even fight.

"MY BEST FRIEND JOSEPHINE JAMES"
by Janet A Smith

My best friend Josephine James
Has called me horrible names.
I know that it's true
Because she told Betty Drew
Who told Ermintrude Jones
Who told Mildred Magrew
Who told Fatima Pugh
Who told ME
That Josephine called me some names.

Oh I'm cross with Josephine James
So I shall call HER some names,
Like Freckly Frump
Grumbly Grump
Or Lumpetty Lump
Or Silly Old Chump!
Can you think of horrible names
For my best friend Josephine James?

Enter two children who sing

"ANYTHING YOU CAN DO" from "Annie Get Your Gun"
by Irving Berlin.

NARRATOR

Some children do not have any friends. Usually it is not because they do not want any friends but perhaps because they are very shy. They are usually very lonely and would like to have friends. There are many ways in which we can help these lonely children. We can ask them to join in our games, choose them as partners and chat with them.

NARRATOR

People who have good friends are very fortunate. There are often times when other people need our love and help. There is an old proverb that says "A friend in need is a friend indeed". There are many occasions when people need a friend or neighbour and are grateful for whatever help is offered. Our neighbours are usually the people who live near us because they are the people we are most likely to be able to help. They may be old and lonely and in need of someone to talk to. They may be ill and unable to get to the shops. We should all try to be good neighbours.

All sing

"NEIGHBOURS" by Tony Hatch

Friends and Neighbours

PAGES 11&12

NARRATOR

Jesus said, "The most important commandment is to love the Lord your God with all your heart, with all your soul, with all your mind, with all your strength. The second most important command is this: Love your neighbour as yourself." When someone asked Jesus who his neighbour was, He told the story of the Good Samaritan.

Children act the following poem

NARRATOR

A man walked along the road to Jericho
He travelled all alone.
Thieves attacked him and he was left to die
And all his money had gone.

There came a certain priest that way
With many problems on his mind,
He passed him by on the other side
For someone else to find.

Then a second traveller came that way,
He stopped to see him there;
But he thought of the danger and hurried on
He didn't seem to care.

At last a Samaritan came along,
With feeling and compassion,
He stopped and tended the wounded man
And carried him to an inn.

All sing

Suggested Hymn: "WHEN I NEEDED A NEIGHBOUR" (TTS)

NARRATOR

There is an organisation called The Samaritans which helps people who are in trouble. When they receive a telephone call, they answer with the words, "The Samaritans–can I help you?" The people who are part of this organisation spend much of their spare time patiently listening to and befriending people who often have no one else to turn to. They are the sort of people who could not turn their backs on someone in difficulty.

All sing

"BRIDGE OVER TROUBLED WATER"
as sung by Simon and Garfunkel.

PRAYER

Dear God we thank You for all our friends.
Help us to care for them and share with them.
Help us to make friends with those children who are lonely.
May we be true friends and only do to others
The things that we would have them do to us.
Be with us, O God, as a special friend throughout our lives.   AMEN

All sing

"WITH A LITTLE HELP FROM MY FRIENDS"
as sung by The Beatles (A)

Harvest — PAGE 1

ATTAINMENT TARGETS
ENGLISH: AT1 Speaking and listening: Levels 1, 2a, 2d, 2e, 4, 5d, 6b, 6c.
AT2 Reading: Levels 3a. 4a.

CHARACTERS

Up to 8 Narrators	Miller	Children to recite
Red Hen	Baker	"Thoughts From a Kitchen"
Cat	Pharaoh	Chorus
Rat	Butler	Prayer Leader
Pig	Joseph	

NARRATOR

The Harvest Festival is one of the most widespread and ancient of religious festivals. Even people who lived in ancient times knew that we all need food to live and that is why they celebrated harvest as a religious occasion. Until a few hundred years ago, most people had only the food they produced for themselves. Most of them lived in villages and worked on the farms.
It was hard work from the time the seeds were planted to the time the crops were harvested and therefore it was expected that everyone would help.

All children sing

"WE PLOUGH THE FIELDS AND SCATTER" (TTS)

Harvest — PAGE 2

NARRATOR

Once upon a time, there was a little red hen who lived in a farmyard. **(Enter Red Hen, a Cat, a Rat and a Pig)** One day the hen found some grains of wheat and took them to the other animals in the farmyard. **(Red Hen acts out the story)**

RED HEN

Who will help me to plant these grains of wheat?

CAT

Not I.

RAT

Not I.

PIG

Not I.

RED HEN

Then I shall plant the seeds myself.

Harvest — PAGE 3

NARRATOR

The little red hen planted the seeds and every day she went to the field to watch the grains of wheat growing. They grew tall and strong. When the little red hen saw that the wheat was ready to be cut, she went to the other animals in the farmyard.

RED HEN

Who will help me to cut the wheat?

CAT

Not I.

RAT

Not I.

PIG

Not I.

RED HEN

Then I shall cut the wheat myself. **(Cuts the wheat)** The wheat is now ready to be made into flour.

Harvest — PAGE 4

NARRATOR

The little red hen took the wheat to the animals in the farmyard.

RED HEN

Who will help me to take the wheat to the mill, to be ground into flour?

CAT

Not I.

RAT

Not I.

PIG

Not I.

RED HEN

Then I shall take the wheat to the mill myself.

NARRATOR

The little red hen took the wheat to the mill **(Enter Miller)** and the miller ground it into flour. The little red hen took the flour to the other animals in the farmyard.

Harvest — PAGE 5

RED HEN
Who will help me to take this flour to the baker, to be made into bread?

CAT
Not I.

RAT
Not I.

PIG
Not I.

RED HEN
Then I shall take the flour to the baker myself.

NARRATOR
The little red hen took the flour to the baker **(Enter Baker)** and when he had made it into bread, she took it to the other animals in the farmyard.

RED HEN
The bread is now ready to be eaten. Who will help me to eat the bread?

Harvest — PAGE 6

CAT
I will.

RAT
I will.

PIG
I will.

RED HEN
No you will not. I shall eat it by myself.

NARRATOR
So she did and the other animals in the farmyard felt hungry as they watched the little red hen eating the delicious bread.

All exit

Harvest

PAGE 7

NARRATOR

In the story, the Little Red Hen did not share the bread with the other animals in the farmyard because they had not shared in the work. However, harvest is one time of the year when we think about those less fortunate than ourselves by sharing with them the fruits of the earth. This way, the whole community can share in the rejoicing as they did in the days when the crops were harvested by hand. Everyone who had helped felt pleased and thankful when the last sheaf was collected. They celebrated with a great feast at which they all had plenty to eat and drink and afterwards they sang songs and danced.

All children sing

"BRINGING IN THE SHEAVES" (SSS)

NARRATOR

Festivals to celebrate harvest are held, at different times, all over the world. In the United States of America people attend Thanksgiving services in church. It is a time to give thanks for peace and plenty. It is a happy occasion when members of a family get together and share the traditional Thanksgiving Day dinner of roast turkey with cranberry sauce followed by pumpkin pie.

Harvest

PAGE 8

NARRATOR

The Jewish religion has two harvest festivals. The first is known as the Feast of Pentecost and celebrates the early wheat harvest. The other celebrates the gathering of fruit and is called the Feast of Tabernacles.

NARRATOR

In Australia and New Zealand harvest festivals are much the same as in Britain. Japan has an important Autumn festival, called the New Taste Festival. The first fruits of the harvest are presented by the Emperor at a special altar. Most religions in both Africa and India have thanksgiving festivals for good harvests. Holi, a Hindu festival, is very popular in Northern India and celebrates the spring wheat harvest.

Suggested Hymn: "COME, YE THANKFUL PEOPLE, COME" (TTS)

NARRATOR

There are many parts of the world, particularly in Africa and Asia where the harvest is never good and sometimes there is none at all. This can be caused by drought, a long period with no rain, or by floods which sweep away all the crops. If the harvest fails there is famine, as in the story of Joseph.

Harvest

PAGE 9

NARRATOR

One day, Pharaoh, the King of Egypt, had a strange dream.

Enter Pharaoh and his butler

PHARAOH

I've had two very strange dreams. I wonder who could tell me what they mean?

BUTLER

I remember when I was in prison with the baker, we both had strange dreams one night. There was a young Hebrew called Joseph in prison with us and he explained the true meaning of our dreams.

PHARAOH

Bring this Joseph to me. **(Exit Butler. Pharaoh paces up and down)** The strangest of dreams. What can they mean? **(Sits down to think)**

Enter Butler with Joseph

PHARAOH

I've had two dreams and the butler says that you will be able to tell me the meaning of them.

Harvest

PAGE 10

JOSEPH

I will try, with the help of God.

PHARAOH

I dreamt that I was standing by a river and seven fat, healthy cows came up out of the water. Seven thin cows came up the river bank and it seemed that the thin cows ate the fat ones. The second dream was about seven fat ears of corn and seven thin ears of corn. The seven thin ears seemed to eat up the seven fat ones. I told this to my magicians but none of them knew what it meant.

JOSEPH

The two dreams have the same meaning. God is showing you what he is about to do. The seven fat cows and the seven plump ears of corn are seven good years. The seven thin cows and the seven thin ears are seven years of famine. Egypt is going to have seven years of plenty followed by seven years of famine.

PHARAOH

What shall we do then?

Harvest

PAGE 11

JOSEPH

I think the best thing to do would be to build great barns during the years of plenty. You can put all the extra corn that you do not need into them.
When the seven years of famine come there will be enough food stored in the barns for your people to eat.

PHARAOH

I would like you to be in charge of all the food in Egypt. My people must do what you tell them.
(Places his ring on Joseph's finger and places a gold chain around his neck)

NARRATOR

Everything happened just as Joseph had said it would. During the seven years of famine in Egypt, Joseph was able to keep the country from starving.

All children sing

"ANY DREAM WILL DO" from "Joseph and his Amazing Technicolour Dreamcoat" by Tim Rice and Andrew Lloyd Webber.

Harvest

PAGE 12

NARRATOR

We have a vast range of food available to us today. We only need to go as far as the local supermarket to buy food from all over the world; bananas from The West Indies, rice from The United States or spices from The Far East. This means that we can have a healthy and varied diet. However, there are many people in the world who are always hungry and lack any variety in their meagre diet.

All children sing

"FOOD GLORIOUS FOOD" from "Oliver"

NARRATOR

A nourishing, varied diet is necessary to keep us healthy. However, it is important that we don't become too preoccupied with food. It is better that we eat to live rather than live to eat.

Harvest — PAGE 13

1 or more children recite poem "THOUGHTS FROM A KITCHEN" by Mary Ormsby

> When I am busy cooking, I sometimes like to think
> That Jesus loved His children, and gave them food and drink;
> He fed them on the mountain, and He fed them by the sea,
> And we are all His children, and He cares for you and me.
>
> When Jesus raised the little girl the people thought was dead,
> He told them not to question her, but give her food instead;
> He always was concerned His friends should have enough to eat;
> But He taught them that the life was more important than the meat.
>
> He told us not to worry overmuch about our food,
> For our Father, in His wisdom, will give us what is good;
> So we may put our trust in Him, and try to do the best
> With the food that He has given us; and He will do the rest.
>
> So if I find my mind is too concerned with earthly bread,
> Then I must try to turn my thoughts to heavenly food instead;
> For Jesus was the Son of God and died for you and me–
> And He cooked His friends their breakfast on the shores of Galilee.

Harvest — PAGE 14

PRAYER

> We thank You God for all the gifts of harvest time.
> For food, fuel and all the natural resources of the earth.
> We are thankful to those who have worked to give us these gifts and for the weather which makes things grow.
> Help us to remember all those who do not have enough to eat and those who are starving.
> May we help by sharing whatever we can with others in the hope that one day they will be as fortunate as we are.
>
> AMEN

All children sing

"THE FIELDS ARE WHITE" written by M.A. Baughen (A)

War and Peace — PAGE 1

> **ATTAINMENT TARGETS**
> ENGLISH: AT1 Speaking and listening: Levels 1, 2a, 2d, 2e, 4, 5d, 6b, 6c.
> AT2 Reading: Levels 3a, 4a.
> AT3 Writing: Levels 2, 3, 4, 5, 6.

CHARACTERS

Up to 9 Narrators
Children to read
  "Letters from the Trenches"
Evacuees including
  Faith
  John
  Anne
  Stan
  Joe
  Mr. Rogers
  Chorus

Crowd of local people including
  Butcher
  Mrs Bulmer
  Mr Phillips
  Mrs Lacey
  Mr Bulmer
  Mrs Richardson
  Mrs Lambert
  A.R.P. Warden
  Mr Jenkins
  Mrs Pennington-Brown
  Mr Pennington-Brown

NARRATOR

"THE FIELDS OF FLANDERS" by Edith Nesbit

Last year the fields were all glad and gay
With silver daisies and silver may;
There were kingcups gold by the river's edge
And primrose stars under every hedge.

This year the fields are trampled and brown,
The hedges are broken and beaten down,
And where the primroses used to grow
Are little black crosses set in a row.

War and Peace — PAGE 2

And the flower of hopes, and the flowers of dreams,
The noble, fruitful, beautiful schemes,
The tree of life with its fruit and bud,
Are trampled down in the mud and the blood.

The changing seasons will bring again
The magic of spring to our wood and plain:
Though the spring be so green as never was seen
The crosses will still be black in the green.

NARRATOR

In the fields of Flanders, during the First World War, hundreds of thousands of brave men fought and died. In the late summer of 1914 the peoples of Britain, France, Russia, Belgium and later Italy found themselves at war with Germany, Austria and Turkey. Completely unaware of the horrors to come and convinced that the war would be over by Christmas, the British marched off to battle in France and Belgium. They were cheered on their way by patriotic and cheerful songs.

All children sing

"PACK UP YOUR TROUBLES IN YOUR OLD KIT BAG"
by George Asaf

War and Peace PAGE 3

NARRATOR

The soldiers had no idea they were going to fight a war in which massed machine guns, heavy artillery, air raids, poison gas, flame throwers, and armoured tanks would be used. The first weeks of fighting with these new weapons made the movements of the armies so dangerous that they were forced to dig trenches for shelter. The trenches were about two metres deep. Wooden duck boards were laid on the bottom of the trench but failed to keep the soldiers' feet out of the mud. The walls were lined with wood, wire netting and sandbags to stop them collapsing in the rain and shellfire. They had to be repaired constantly. Trench conditions were appalling.

"**Letter from the Trenches**"

Children can research conditions in the trenches, imagine they are soldiers and write letters home to their families. These can be read aloud

Suggested Hymns: "O GOD OUR HELP IN AGES PAST" (SOP)
"FATHER HEAR THE PRAYER WE OFFER"
(MHB)

War and Peace PAGE 4

NARRATOR

About 14 million people–soldiers and civilians–died in the First World War. People hoped it would be the war to end all wars, but in 1939 it became obvious that this was not to be.

(An extract from "1940" by John Betjeman)

As I lay in the bath the air was filling with bells;
Over the steam of the window, out in the sun,
From the village below came hoarsely the patriot yells
And I knew that the next World War had at last begun.

NARRATOR

World War Two was total warfare. It raged across almost all of Europe, North Africa, China, South-East Asia and all the oceans of the world. During the Second World War, the development of heavy artillery and bomber aircraft meant that no civilian town or village was safe from attack. From September 1940 to May 1941, German planes bombed London nearly every night. It was called "The Blitz". Because innocent children were in danger, they were evacuated from the large cities and moved into the countryside. Those who were sent away had to leave the people they loved most and live among strangers, sometimes for years.

War and Peace — PAGE 5

NARRATOR

The evacuation started at the beginning of September. People did not have to send their children away but by the end of the first week in September, three-quarters of a million school children had left the cities of Britain. These children were known as evacuees. They left home carrying a gas mask in a box and a few of their treasured possessions in suitcases, carrier bags and rucksacks.
When the children reached the countryside they were allocated to their new homes or billets. The children were taken to the town or village hall and the local people chose which children they were going to look after.   **(Exit Narrators)**

Enter Mr Phillips who sits at a table. A noisy crowd of local people enter and gather round the table. The evacuees enter looking very frightened. They stay very close to their teacher, Mr Rogers

The local people begin shouting their demands to Mr Phillips

MRS LACEY

I'd like that pretty little girl with the red bow in her hair, Mr Phillips.

MR PHILLIPS

I'm the billeting officer, Mrs Lacey. You must wait your turn like everyone else.

War and Peace — PAGE 6

MR BULMER

I want at least two strong, healthy children to help out on the farm.

MR PHILLIPS

Just wait a minute, Mr Bulmer. We've got to do this properly.

MRS RICHARDSON

I'd like an older child to help with my young children.

BUTCHER

Somebody who can ride a bicycle to deliver the meat to my customers.

MRS LAMBERT

No boys.

MRS BULMER

No girls.

A.R.P. WARDEN

Must be smart, tidy and punctual.

War and Peace

PAGE 7

MR JENKINS

Can't stand noisy children. Must be quiet.

MR PHILLIPS

(**Bangs the table loudly**) Quiet! Will you all please be quiet. This is getting us nowhere. I'll allocate the children when you all quieten down. Could the teacher in charge organise these children into some sort of order?

MR ROGERS

All right children. Get into a line but stay in your family groups and face the front.

When the children are lined up, the local people walk round them and select some of them. Faith, John, Anne, Stan and Joe remain. The rest of the children exit in small groups with the local people

FAITH

(**To Mr Rogers**) Please Sir, what's going to happen to us, Sir?

MR ROGERS

Don't worry Faith. Mr Phillips will find a family for you. (**Looks at his watch**) I'll have to go now, my train leaves in ten minutes. Take care and don't forget to keep in touch. Goodbye children. (**Exit**)

War and Peace

PAGE 8

ANNE

Who's going to take us, Mr Phillips?

MR PHILLIPS

There should be some more people on the way.

ANNE

We all want to stay together.

STAN

We all live in the same street, you see.

FAITH

You won't let them split us up, will you? Our John won't go to sleep at night until I've told him a story.

MR PHILLIPS

You'll be all right. Just wait and see. I'll go and see if there is anyone else on the way. You wait here. I won't be long. (**Exit**)

JOHN

(**Crying**) I want to go home Faith. Nobody wants us. I want to go home to our Mum and Dad.

War and Peace

PAGE 9

FAITH

Don't cry, don't cry John. We've got to stay here where it's safe. It's going to be a bit like being on holiday. There will be lots of new places to explore.

STAN

What, like cowsheds and pigsties? I can't see that being much fun.

JOE

I've seen plenty of trees we could climb and scarecrows for target practice. Have you brought your catapult, John?

JOHN

No, I just want to go home.

ANNE

Oh come on John, cheer up. We might get to live with a shopkeeper, perhaps someone with a sweetshop. You'd like that wouldn't you?

JOHN

No, I just want to go home.

War and Peace

PAGE 10

FAITH

I'm going to look after you now John, just like Mum did. Now stop crying, no-one is going to want a cry-baby.

STAN

Quiet everybody. I think there's someone coming.

Enter Mr Phillips with Mr and Mrs Pennington-Brown

MR PHILLIPS

Now children, this is Mr and Mrs Pennington-Brown. **(To Mr and Mrs Pennington-Brown)** These are the children I've been telling you about. They want to stay together as a group. What do you think?

MRS PENNINGTON-BROWN

I don't think that will be a problem. They'd be very welcome if they would like to live with us. We've plenty of room.

JOHN

I want to go home.

MR PENNINGTON-BROWN

Then home you will go. Everyone into the car.

War and Peace — PAGE 11

JOHN

CAR! Car did you say? Come on everyone. A car! **(John rushes off followed by the rest of the children, Mr and Mrs Pennington-Brown and Mr Phillips)**

NARRATOR

The children sometimes found it very difficult to settle into their new homes but at least they were safe from constant bombings and life in air-raid shelters. The death toll of World War Two was much higher than that of World War One. Approximately 55 million people, military and civilians, died.

All children sing

"THE LAST FAREWELL" as sung by Roger Whittaker

NARRATOR

In Britain, all those who died in wartime fighting for their country are remembered on Armistice Day, which was first celebrated in 1918 at the end of the First World War. Armistice Day is the 11th of November but the nearest Sunday to this is called Remembrance Sunday. On this day, wreathes of poppies are laid on war memorials and in gardens of remembrance throughout the country. The red poppy was chosen for these wreaths because of a poem written during the First World War.

War and Peace — PAGE 12

(An Extract from "IN FLANDERS FIELDS" by John Mcrae)

In Flanders fields the poppies grow
Between the crosses row on row,
   That mark our place; and in the sky
   The larks, still bravely singing, fly
Scarce heard amid the guns below.

All children sing

"WHERE HAVE ALL THE FLOWERS GONE?" as sung by Pete Seeger (A)

NARRATOR

On Remembrance Day, people wear red poppies to remember those who died in wartime. The proceeds from the sale of the poppies go to help those disabled by war. War causes immense suffering and sorrow. How much better the world would be if we could live together in peace.

"PRAYER OF ST. FRANCIS" (Can be spoken or sung) (A)

NARRATOR

Jesus said, "As I have loved you so must you love one another." John Lennon tried to imagine what the world would be like if all people were to put these words into practice.

All children sing

"IMAGINE" by John Lennon

Energy

PAGE 1

ATTAINMENT TARGETS
SCIENCE: AT13 Energy: Levels 4b, 4c, 5, 6a, 6d, 7c.
ENGLISH: AT1 Speaking and Listening: Levels 1, 2a, 2d, 2e, 4, 5d, 6b, 6c.
AT2 Reading: 3a, 4a.

CHARACTERS

Sun	Judy Joule	Professor Solar
Corn	Professor Coal	Professor Water
Chicken	Professor Gas	Professor Wind
Farmer	Professor Oil	The Potentials–
Seed	Professor Nuclear	a group of dancers
Grass	Narrator	Sherlock Holmes
Cow	Announcer	Chorus

NARRATOR

Everything that changes or moves involves energy in some form or another. People depend on energy in many ways – it is what makes things happen. Energy is vital to the world and all the people who live in it. It is never destroyed or created; it is only changed from one form to another. The sun produces tremendous amounts of energy, some of which is captured by the earth.

Enter Sun. Skips around

Children sing

"THE SUN HAS GOT HIS HAT ON"

Energy

PAGE 2

SUN

I shine down on the earth every day. My strong rays pour out light and warmth, which we usually take for granted. Think what it would be like if I wasn't here. In a cold dark world, plants would not grow. If there were no plants there would be no food for animals. If there were no plants or animals you would not survive. The earth would be a dead, empty wasteland, without energy from me. I am always there even when you can't see me. I shall probably be around for a lot longer. My energy is renewable; let me show you what I mean.

Enter Corn, Chicken, Farmer, Seed, Grass, Cow

SUN

I am the sun. I shine down on the seed which grows into corn.

CORN

I am the corn which grows from the seed. I am picked and scattered for the chicken to eat.

CHICKEN

I am the chicken and I eat the corn, that grew from the energy, that came from the sun. I lay eggs for the farmer to eat.

Energy

PAGE 3

FARMER

    I am the farmer and I have eaten the egg which the chicken laid, which ate the corn, which grew from the seed, which the sun shone down on.

SUN

    I am the sun, I shine down on the seed.

SEED

    I am the seed that the sun shone down on, and I grow into grass.

GRASS

    I am the grass that the cow eats, that grew from the seed, that the sun shone down on. I get my energy from the light that shines from the sun.

COW

    I am the cow that ate the grass, that grew from the seed, that the sun shone down on.

SUN

    Now you can see how much you depend on me for your energy.

Suggested Hymns: "SOMEBODY GREATER" (CAP)
                       "THINK OF A WORLD" (TTS)

Energy

PAGE 4

All exit

Enter Announcer

ANNOUNCER

    We are going over to Channel 10's "Discussion Time", which this week will examine the energy problem. Meet your host for tonight's show; Judy Joule.

Enter Judy Joule to applause

JUDY JOULE

    Thank you, thank you. This audience gets better every day. Welcome to tonight's show on the energy problem. On tonight's show we have some very important people in the energy business: Professor Coal, Professor Gas, Professor Oil and Professor Nuclear. **(Enter Professor Coal, Professor Gas, Professor Oil and Professor Nuclear who sit facing the audience)** At present a very important energy source is provided by fossil fuels. However, will this always be the case?
    (Turns to Professor Coal) Good evening Professor Coal. Could you begin by explaining the development of fossil fuels?

Energy

PAGE 5

PROFESSOR COAL

Many millions of years ago a great deal of the energy that made plants and animals was not used; instead it was stored underground for us to use. Coal is a fossil fuel, formed from plants that grew millions of years ago. Oil and gas were formed from the remains of plants and animals that once lived in the sea.

JUDY JOULE

I understand that fewer people are using coal to heat their homes. Does this mean there is less demand for coal?

PROFESSOR COAL

Not at all. About 20% of the world's energy comes from coal and its use is increasing. The main problem is that we have only enough reserves to make it an important source of energy for another two to three hundred years.

JUDY JOULE

That's very worrying, isn't it?

PROFESSOR COAL

Yes, but if people start to save energy it would last a lot longer.

Energy

PAGE 6

PROFESSOR OIL

The same thing applies to oil.

JUDY JOULE

How long do you think oil supplies are going to last?

PROFESSOR OIL

Just about 40 more years.

JUDY JOULE

Well, maybe that's good, because oil slicks have been known to destroy sea life.

PROFESSOR OIL

That may be true, but oil spills don't happen very often. We need oil and that's all that matters to people in the oil business. You may ask why do we need oil? We need oil to produce heat, to make other useful substances such as plastics and as the main fuel for transport. These are just a few examples of the many uses of oil.

JUDY JOULE

Now, what about gas? According to the information I have here **(looks at clipboard)** there are less than sixty years of natural gas reserves remaining.

Energy — PAGE 7

PROFESSOR GAS

I'm afraid your information is correct. This is very unfortunate because natural gas is a clean fuel. It contains no sulphur which is one of the main causes of acid rain. However, the gas which is piped into the gas mains and delivered to houses and factories is made up almost entirely of methane. It's possible to produce methane from household rubbish so even when the reserves of natural gas run out, there will still be ways of producing gas.

JUDY JOULE

(To the audience) That may be so but we do seem to have an energy crisis on our hands. Have we a solution? What about nuclear power? (To Professor Nuclear) Professor Nuclear, many people say that the Sun is the only safe nuclear reactor, because it is one hundred and fifty million kilometres away. Would you like to comment on this?

PROFESSOR NUCLEAR

There are about three hundred and fifty nuclear power stations around the world. They supply almost 20% of the world's electricity. Nuclear power is a much "cleaner" way of producing power. Unlike power stations using coal or oil, nuclear power does not contribute to environmental problems such as acid rain and the greenhouse effect.

Energy — PAGE 8

JUDY JOULE

This may be so but it is a fact that the large amounts of radioactive waste created by the nuclear process can't be destroyed. Some of it is so dangerous that it must be isolated for hundreds of thousands of years. There is also a risk of a nuclear accident like the one in 1986 at Chernobyl in the USSR.
(To the audience) Surely, what we must look for is a safe and environmentally friendly source of power which is renewable. Before we speak to our second panel of experts, we'll take a short break while you enjoy stored energy at its very best. Ladies and gentlemen, The Potentials!

All exit except Judy Joule who sits to one side

Enter The Potentials, a group of dancers who dance to "HIGH ENERGY" as sung by Evelyn Thomas

JUDY JOULE

My next guests have been working very hard to find alternative forms of energy. Let's give a very warm welcome to Professor Solar, Professor Water and Professor Wind. (Leads audience applause)

Enter Professor Solar, Professor Water and Professor Wind and sit facing the audience

Energy

PAGE 9

JUDY JOULE

Professor Solar, what do you think will be the main source of energy in the future?

PROFESSOR SOLAR

The sun provides the Earth with enormous amounts of energy. Solar panels are used to trap the sun's heat and then the energy from the sun can be used for heating purposes or to produce electricity. Energy provided by the sun is called "solar energy". I believe that solar energy will be the main source of our energy in the long-term future.

JUDY JOULE

Thank you, Professor Solar. Our next guest is Professor Water. Welcome to the programme Professor. Could you tell us about harnessing energy from water?

PROFESSOR WATER

The energy in moving water supplies over 20% of the world's electricity through the use of hydro-electric power stations. These use the energy in moving water to turn one or more turbines which produce the electricity in generators. Other forms of water energy, especially tidal and wave energy, also have great potential. We hope that future research will make energy from water more efficient and less expensive.

Energy

PAGE 10

JUDY JOULE

Thank you Professor Water. That sounds very interesting. Now, moving on to our next guest, Professor Wind. How can energy from wind compete with solar power and water power?

PROFESSOR WIND

I think the wind is one of the most promising energy sources. The most important use of the wind is to produce electricity. The wind is used to turn the blades of a wind turbine which is attached to an electricity generator. Wind power can generate electricity at the same price as fossil fuels and nuclear power. It is also relatively safe and pollution free.

JUDY JOULE

Thank you Professor Wind and many thanks to all our panel this evening. **(To audience)** Tonight's discussion has certainly highlighted the possibility of some very interesting developments in the energy field. Thank you and goodnight.

All exit

All children sing

"WINDMILLS OF MY MIND" as sung by Noel Harrison

Energy

PAGE 11

Enter Announcer

ANNOUNCER

In this century we have helped ourselves to an enormous amount of our energy resources. We are now aware that if we continue to use them at the present rate, our main sources of energy could soon be used up. How then can we save energy? Let us investigate inside our homes. Over to Sherlock Holmes.

Props brought on to signify rooms in a house

Enter Sherlock Holmes carrying a large magnifying glass

SHERLOCK HOLMES

I will begin my investigation in the lounge. Ah, double glazing, a very economical means of keeping heat in the home and reducing heating costs. Very sensible, a comfortable armchair next to the fire and a sweater nearby. A quick check, good, no appliances left on. Into the kitchen now. A lot of energy is used here. A microwave oven is a very energy efficient way of cooking food. There's a bowl in the sink, excellent, washing under a running tap would use far more hot water. Energy saved there. Lids on all the pans means that no heat will be lost during cooking. A washing machine with half load facility, another saving. Fridge well away from the radiator, good planning. Now, into the bathroom. Wonderful, a shower, that will use much less water than the bath. The bedrooms, not much energy used there, they are all asleep!

Energy

PAGE 12

And so, finally, to the loft. Ah, excellent, the loft is fully insulated, keeping heat in the home rather than letting it out into the sky. A truly energy-conscious family. Certainly doing their bit to help to conserve energy.

ANNOUNCER

That is the end of tonight's programmes. We will close our transmission with the end of evening prayer. Thank You God for the supplies of coal, gas and oil that are here for us to use. Thank You that they help to make our lives more comfortable, giving us light where there would be darkness and heat where there would be cold. Help us to appreciate all the benefits which energy brings and give us the good sense to use them wisely.

AMEN.

Communications   PAGE 1

ATTAINMENT TARGETS
SCIENCE: AT12 The scientific aspects of information technology including microelectronics: Levels 1, 2a, 2b, 3b, 4a.
ENGLISH: AT1 Speaking and Listening: Levels 1, 2a, 2d, 2e, 4, 5d, 6b, 6c.
　　　　　AT2 Reading: Levels 3a, 4a.

CHARACTERS

Up to 12 Narrators
1st Nomad
2nd Nomad
2nd Nomad's Wife
3rd Nomad
4th Nomad
Mother
Weather Forecast
Lisa
Speaking Clock
Telephone Engineer
Chorus
Prayer Leader

NARRATOR

The word "communicate" means to send a message. One of the ways in which we communicate is by speaking to someone else. Speech, drawing pictures, dancing and singing were all methods of communication which developed tens of thousands of years ago. Speaking was very important to early people. It was the only way they had of sending messages. It used to be thought that there was only one language at first, and that all other languages started from it. The story of the "Tower of Babel" was the way in which the Bible explained why men of different races or tribes speak different languages.

Communications   PAGE 2

NARRATOR

One day a group of people were wandering across a stretch of wide, flat land between two great rivers. They decided to camp there for a while and pitched their tents. The area they had chosen was eventually to become the site of the city of Babylon.

Enter a group of nomads who sit round a campfire

All sing

"BY THE RIVERS OF BABYLON" as sung by Boney M.

1ST NOMAD

Well, it will soon be time to move on.

2ND NOMAD

Why bother moving on? There is plenty of good grazing land for the animals. Why can't we just stay here?

2ND NOMAD'S WIFE

What a good idea. I'm tired of having to pack everything up and move on. There's plenty of clay and mud here on the river banks. Why don't we build proper houses like we saw in the town?

Communications — PAGE 3

3RD NOMAD

In fact we could build a city here.

4TH NOMAD

A city of our own. That would be wonderful!

All exit

NARRATOR

So it was decided. They made bricks and mortar to hold the bricks together. They all worked together to build houses of baked mud and they soon had a new city.

Enter 2nd and 3rd Nomads

3RD NOMAD

Building with mud bricks is quite easy really. What about building ourselves a temple with a tower? We could keep on building it up and up, higher and higher until its top reaches heaven.

2ND NOMAD

That's right, we could get to where God lives. We could be like him. Come on let's get started.

Exit 2nd and 3rd Nomads

Communications — PAGE 4

NARRATOR

They kept on building the tower higher and higher. God saw what they were doing and realised that they were trying to show how great and clever they were. They were becoming far too proud of themselves, so God decided to make life more difficult for them. He muddled up their speech and made them all speak different languages so that they could not understand one another. They could not go on building the tower in the confusion that followed because they could not tell each other what to do. The people split up and the families went off in different directions, each speaking their own language. The tower became known as the Tower of Babel. "Babel" was connected with the Hebrew word for confusion and came to mean a confused sound of voices. The word "babble", which is more commonly used today, is thought to have come from the word "Babel".

NARRATOR

By using a common language, two or more people can co-operate and help each other. Another form of communication is writing. The first writing was often in picture form. As soon as people could speak and write, they had the problem of how to send messages long distances. They began to send each other letters. The first letters were sent by messengers. They were usually runners, or travelled by horse. Nowadays most of the mail is carried by air and rail.

Communications — PAGE 5

All sing

"PLEASE MISTER POSTMAN!" as sung by The Carpenters

NARRATOR

Modern communications form part of what has become known as information technology. Information technology means the use of science to help people communicate more quickly and easily. It is technology based on the microprocessor or silicon chip. It is now possible to fit a very complicated electrical circuit on to a tiny chip of silicon. The postal service is one of the two major worldwide communications networks that makes use of this invention. The other is the telephone network over which messages are conveyed instantly throughout the world. Dial or press a number and in seconds you can be talking to the person next door or someone on the other side of the world. Your voice travels in the form of electric, radio or light signals. The telephone has become an essential part of modern life for business and personal use.

All sing

"RING, RING WHY DON'T YOU GIVE ME A CALL?" as sung by ABBA

Enter 2 children (Mother and Lisa) each carrying a telephone and sit as far apart as possible.
3 more children (Weather Forecast, Speaking Clock and Telephone Engineer) enter and sit behind a screen

Communications — PAGE 6

MOTHER

Hello? Is that you Lisa? I've been trying to get through for ages. Can you hear a funny buzzing sound on the line?

WEATHER FORECAST

It will be mainly dry, with some outbreaks of rain. Some snow and fog may be expected later, with gales moving in from the West.

MOTHER

Lisa? Lisa? Is that you? Can you hear me?

WEATHER FORECAST

The snow will fall mainly on high ground...

MOTHER

Who's that talking about snow? Where's our Lisa? I want to speak to her. I'm not bothered about the snow, am I? It's Dad I want to talk about.

LISA

Mum? I can hear you Mum. What did you say about Dad?

Communications PAGE 7

SPEAKING CLOCK

At the third stroke the time will be 9.23 precisely.

LISA

A stroke. A stroke you say? Dad's had a stroke?

WEATHER FORECAST

A high pressure area moving in from the Atlantic tomorrow. . .

LISA

High blood pressure? That'll be because he's overweight. You'll have to stop giving him so many chips.

MOTHER

Stroke, blood pressure, chips? What are you talking about, Lisa? There's nothing wrong with your Dad. I rang to tell you that he's got a new job.

SPEAKING CLOCK

At the third stroke it will be 9.23 and 30 seconds.

Communications PAGE 8

MOTHER

Who keeps talking about strokes? I'll be having a stroke in a second if you don't clear the line.

TELEPHONE ENGINEER

Hello, are you having problems, Madam? There seems to be a fault on the line. What number are you calling?

MOTHER

It's Masley 859743.

TELEPHONE ENGINEER

Hey, that's our Lisa's number. Hello Lisa. Is that you? It's your Dad. Did your Mum tell you? I've got a new job.

LISA

Dad? Where are you?

TELEPHONE ENGINEER

At work. I'm the new telephone engineer.

A group of children dance to and sing the chorus of "COMMUNICATION" by Spandau Ballet

Communications PAGE 9

NARRATOR

With the development of the silicon chip, information of many different types can be transmitted through the telephone network. Computers send information to each other, while telex machines send typed messages and fax machines send pictures of documents or illustrations. Other telecommunication systems such as radio and television are also ways of instantly sending words and pictures over long distances. The invention of tape recorders and video recorders made it possible to record and store pictures and sound, which can be played back at any time. Computers also use silicon chips to remember information. Specially organised information stored in a computer is called a "database".

NARRATOR

All forms of communication are important to our everyday lives. However, there is another very important form of communication that is available to us all. This system involves sending thoughts and words to God. It requires no modern technology or electronic devices, only a belief that there is a God and that he hears and answers prayers.

Communications PAGE 10

NARRATOR

"PROOF" by Ethel Romig Fuller.

If radio's slim fingers can pluck a melody
From night–and toss it over a continent or sea;
If the petalled white notes of a violin
Are blown across the mountains or the city's din;
If songs like crimson roses are culled from thin blue air–
Why should mortals wonder if God hears prayer?

Suggested Hymn: "FATHER HEAR THE PRAYER WE OFFER"
(TTS)

NARRATOR

Communication is not always a one-way process of passing on a message to someone else. It often involves listening. However, many people talk too much and never listen to others. As a result, they miss many chances of hearing new and worthwhile ideas.

Communications — PAGE 11

NARRATOR

"THE TELEPHONE" by Michel Quoist.

I have just hung up; why did he telephone?
I don't know...Oh! I get it...
I talked a lot and listened very little.
Forgive me, Lord, it was a monologue and not a dialogue.
I explained my idea and did not get his;
Since I didn't listen, I learned nothing,
Since I didn't listen, it didn't help,
Since I didn't listen, we didn't communicate.
Forgive me, Lord, for we were connected,
and now we are cut off.

NARRATOR

No matter where we live in the world or what our religious beliefs, we never need to be cut off from God. In the Bible God speaks to us, as He speaks nowhere else. God chose to make His message of salvation known by means of the written word–our Old and New Testaments. Jesus often left His friends and went alone to talk to God. He told the people to do the same and to ask for God's help in their prayers. Jesus taught the people the words of a prayer, the one we know as "The Lords Prayer". He told them that this was the prayer He wanted them to say when they talked to God.

Communications — PAGE 12

PRAYER

Our Father, who art in heaven,
Hallowed be Thy name;
Thy kingdom come;
Thy will be done;
on earth as it is in heaven.
Give us this day our daily bread.
And forgive us our trespasses,
As we forgive those who trespass against us
And lead us not into temptation;
but deliver us from evil.

AMEN

All sing

"MY PRAYER" as sung by The Platters

A King is Born

PAGE 1

ATTAINMENT TARGETS
ENGLISH: AT1 Speaking and listening: Levels 1, 2a, 2d, 2e, 4, 5d, 6b, 6c.
AT2 Reading: Levels 3a, 4a.
AT3 Writing: Levels 2a, 3a, 3b, 3d, 3e, 4a, 4c, 4d, 4e, 5b, 5d.

CHARACTERS

Up to 11 Narrators	1st Shepherd	Children to read
Angel Gabriel	2nd Shepherd	Letters to Santa
Mary	3rd Shepherd	Chorus
Joseph	3 Kings	Prayer Leader
Innkeeper		

NARRATOR

The birth of a baby is seen as a gift from God or the gods to a family. Every year when we celebrate our birthday, we look back in wonder to the miracle of our birth, and look forward hopefully to happy days to come. One way of celebrating a birthday is to have a party and invite all our friends to share the happy occasion. It is exciting to receive presents and cards.

Enter a group of children carrying a birthday cake. They stand around the narrator and sing "HAPPY BIRTHDAY"

48

A King is Born

PAGE 2

NARRATOR

Birthdays come in all shapes and sizes. There are very important ones, like a first birthday, that celebrates the baby's first year of life. A hundredth birthday is also very special because it celebrates a century of life. When you are seventeen you can learn to drive and take your driving test. **(Enter child with "L" plates)** At eighteen, you have certain rights including the right to vote. At twenty-one a person officially "comes of age".

Enter group of children celebrating a twenty-first birthday. They throw streamers and sing "TWENTY-ONE TODAY"

NARRATOR

The celebration of the birthday of Jesus Christ is a very special time of the year. Nobody knows at what time of year Jesus was born. Christians who lived a few hundred years after Jesus, chose the twenty-fifth of December to remember his birthday. This day became known as Christmas Day. The word "Christmas" comes from "Christ's Mass"–the special church service which celebrates the birth of Jesus Christ. The build up to such an important event begins weeks before. The four-week period leading up to Christ's birthday is known as Advent which means "coming". This is a time when people are preparing for the greatest coming of all time – the birth of Jesus Christ.

ACTIVE ASSEMBLIES FOR THE NATIONAL CURRICULUM   SCHOFIELD & SIMS LTD

A King is Born — PAGE 3

NARRATOR

Extract from "ADVENT 1955" by John Betjeman.

The Advent bells call out "Prepare,
Your world is journeying to the birth
Of God made Man for us on earth."

"The time draws near the birth of Christ"
A present that cannot be priced
Given two thousand years ago.
Yet if God had not given so
He still would be a distant stranger
And not the Baby in the manger.

All sing

"HARK THE GLAD SOUND!" (SOP)

NARRATOR

One of the most popular customs of Advent is the lighting of the candles on an Advent wreath. The first candle is lit on the first Sunday in Advent. On the second Sunday, it is lit again, and a second one with it. By the fourth Sunday, all the candles have been lit. Many festivals of light take place during the very darkest time of the year. The Jewish and Hindu religions both celebrate festivals of light. These are called Hanukkah and Divali.

A King is Born — PAGE 4

NARRATOR

Early Christians thought about the idea of light and used it as a symbol to explain the meaning of Jesus' birth. In his Gospel John writes that the birth of Jesus is like light coming into the world.
The story of the birth of Jesus is told every year. . .

NARRATOR

"AS JOSEPH WAS A-WALKING" (Anon)

As Joseph was a-walking
  He heard Angels sing,
"This night shall be born
  Our Heavenly King.

"He neither shall be born
  In house nor in hall,
Nor in the place of paradise,
  But in an ox-stall.

"He shall not be clothed
  In purple nor pall;
But all in fair linen,
  As wear babies all.

"He shall not be rocked
  In silver nor gold,
But in a wooden cradle
  That rocks on the mould.

"He neither shall be christened
  In milk nor in wine,
But in pure spring-well water
  Fresh spring from Bethine."

A King is Born

PAGE 5

All children sing

"WHEN A CHILD IS BORN" as sung by Johnny Mathis

Enter Mary who sits down and begins to sew

Enter Angel Gabriel. Mary looks surprised

GABRIEL

Don't be frightened, Mary. I am the Angel Gabriel, a messenger from God and I've brought some good news. Soon you will have a baby boy. You must call Him Jesus. He will be great. He will be The Son of God. **(Exit)**

Enter Joseph

MARY

Joseph, I have just had a message from God. I am going to have a baby boy and we must call Him Jesus. I can't understand why God has chosen me.

JOSEPH

What marvellous news, Mary. We are very fortunate to have been chosen. You know we must leave Nazareth and go to Bethlehem to be taxed. Do you think you will be well enough to make the journey?

A King is Born

PAGE 6

MARY

Is it far to Bethlehem?

JOSEPH

Yes, but we will take the journey slowly. My donkey is steady, and you will not have to walk. **(Both exit)**

All sing

"LITTLE DONKEY" (CGC)

NARRATOR

After a long tiring journey Mary and Joseph reached Bethlehem.

All sing

"O LITTLE TOWN OF BETHLEHEM" (First verse only) (TTS)

NARRATOR

Bethlehem was crowded and all the inns were full.

Enter Mary and Joseph

MARY

We must find somewhere to rest soon. I am very tired.

A King is Born — PAGE 7

JOSEPH

Here's an inn we haven't tried yet. Perhaps they'll have room for us.   **(They knock on the door of the inn. Innkeeper enters)**   Have you a room, please, for my wife and . . .

INNKEEPER

I'm sorry, the inn is already full.

JOSEPH

Is there anywhere we can rest? My wife is going to have a baby.

MARY

I'm so tired, anything will do.

INNKEEPER

The only place I can think of is the stable. It's warm and dry but you'll have to share it with the animals.

JOSEPH

That will do. Thank you so much.

INNKEEPER

Come this way.   **(Leads them to the stable. All exit)**

A King is Born — PAGE 8

All sing

"SILENT NIGHT" (MHB)

Stable scene with Mary, Joseph and the baby

Enter shepherds who kneel in front of the crib and recite
"THE SHEPHERDS' CAROL" (Anon)

1ST SHEPHERD

> We stood on the hills, Lady,
> Our day's work done,
> Watching the frosted meadows
> That winter had won.

2ND SHEPHERD

> The evening was calm, Lady,
> The air so still,
> Silence more lovely than music
> Folded the hill.

3RD SHEPHERD

> There was a star, Lady,
> Shone in the night,
> Larger than Venus it was
> And bright, so bright.

A King is Born — PAGE 9

2ND SHEPHERD

> Oh, a voice from the sky, Lady,
> It seemed to us then
> Telling of God being born
> In the world of men.

1ST SHEPHERD

> And so we have come, Lady,
> Our day's work done,
> Our love, our hopes, ourselves
> We give to your son.

3RD SHEPHERD

> Here is my coat to keep Him warm.

2ND SHEPHERD

> Here is a lamb with my love.

1ST SHEPHERD

> I only have my staff. I'm sorry, it doesn't seem like much of a present but I will serve Him for all my life.

All sing

"AWAY IN A MANGER" (MHB)

A King is Born — PAGE 10

NARRATOR

> Following the same star that the shepherds had seen, three kings visited King Herod at his palace in Jerusalem. They were searching for the newborn King of the Jews. Herod told them a Messiah, a Saviour, was expected to be born in Bethlehem. They continued to follow the star until it stopped over the stable.

Enter 3 Kings with gifts of gold, frankincense and myrrh which are given during the following carol

All sing

"WE THREE KINGS" (WCV)

NARRATOR

> Ever since that time, people all over the world have remembered Jesus' birthday. They have been joyful as the shepherds were and they have also given presents. The act of giving is an important part of the Christmas festival. God gave himself to mankind in the form of His son. The three Kings gave their gifts to the baby Jesus. People give each other Christmas presents and Father Christmas leaves presents for children. When we give a present to someone we also give a little bit of ourselves.

All sing

"TWELVE DAYS OF CHRISTMAS" (CC)

A King is Born — PAGE 11

NARRATOR

Many children write a letter to Santa Claus or Father Christmas about the presents they would like for Christmas.

The children can read their own letters to Santa. These should express wishes for things that money cannot buy

Dear Santa

Thank you for the lovely presents you brought me last year. This Christmas do you think you could bring my mum an extra pair of hands please. We have at least ten people for Christmas dinner and every year mum says "I wish I had another pair of hands."

Hope you like the mince pie I baked especially for you. Beware of the dog. He gets angry when he's disturbed during the night.

Love from

A King is Born — PAGE 12

PRAYER

Thank You Lord for happy days especially birthdays and Christmas.
Thank You for the many gifts and all the special things to eat and drink.
Amidst all the excitement, help us to remember You on your birthday.
Help us also to remember that it is better to give than to receive.
This Christmas comfort those who have no presents, those who are short of food and those who will be sad because someone they love will not be with them.
Thank You Lord Jesus that I can remember your birthday each year.
And for filling my heart with joy.

AMEN

All sing

"HARK! THE HERALD ANGELS SING" (MHB)

China

PAGE 1

ATTAINMENT TARGETS
ENGLISH: AT1 Speaking and listening: Levels 1, 2a, 2d, 2e, 4, 5d, 6b.
                  AT2 Reading: Levels 3a, 4a.
TECHNOLOGY: AT1 Identifying needs and opportunities: Levels 2c, 3b, 4a, 4f, 5a, 6a.
                         AT2 Generating a design: Levels 1, 2a, 3, 4, 5a, 5b, 5c, 5d, 6a, 6c.
                         AT3 Planning and making: Levels 2a, 2b, 2c, 3, 4b, 4c, 4d, 4e, 5.
                         AT4 Evaluating: Levels 2a, 3a, 3b, 4a, 4b, 5a, 5b.

CHARACTERS

Up to 7 Narrators	Children with kites	3rd god's voice
Teacher	Dragon children	12 animals
Up to 12 Pupils	1st god's voice	Chorus
Chinese Narrator	2nd god's voice	Prayer Leader

Enter 3 Narrators

NARRATOR

The People's Republic of China is the third largest country in the world, after the USSR and Canada. More people live in China than in any other country on earth. It is the home of more than one billion or 1000 million people.

Suggested Hymn: "I BELONG TO A FAMILY" by Karl Dallas (TTS)

China

PAGE 2

NARRATOR

There are many differences between China and Britain. A major difference is the language which has no alphabet but a complicated system of thousands of characters. **(Two children enter with a banner showing large Chinese characters and an explanation of the meaning)** Each of these characters has to be learnt, which is a difficult task for children at school.

NARRATOR

There are also differences in the calendar. From the beginning of the twentieth century, China adopted the same calendar as Western nations. However, the old calendar based on the phases of the Moon is still an important part of Chinese life and the reason behind many ancient customs. The lunar (or Moon) calendar begins with the Chinese New Year. This begins on day one of the first lunar month–between late January and mid February and it lasts for fifteen days. Most people get three days holiday and schools close for two weeks.

China — PAGE 3

NARRATOR

Chinese people give each new year the name of an animal. This, for example, is the year of the...

Horse	1990	2002
Goat	1991	2003
Monkey	1992	2004
Cockerel	1993	2005
Dog	1994	2006
Pig	1995	2007
Rat	1996	2008
Ox	1997	2009
Tiger	1998	2010
Hare	1999	2011
Dragon	2000	2012
Snake	2001	2013

Here is one of the stories about how this custom began. It has been told for thousands of years. The old year was nearly over.

Enter Dragon, Monkey, Horse, Pig, Snake, Cockerel, Rat, Ox, Hare, Tiger, Goat and Dog. The children can wear animal masks.

NARRATOR

The animals waited eagerly for the new year to begin. This one was going to be particularly interesting, for the gods had decided to give it a name. Even better, they were going to name it after one of the animals. But which animal would it be? They all had their own ideas about that!

China — PAGE 4

DRAGON

I am the most terrifying of you all. Give my name to the year; call it "the Year of the Dragon".

MONKEY

Look what I can do. **(Perform some acrobatics)** Name the new year after me; name it "the Year of the Monkey".

HORSE

Name it after me. See how elegant and fine and strong I am. **(Horse rears and snorts proudly)**

PIG

No, name it after me.

SNAKE

After me.

COCKEREL

After me.

RAT

No, me.

China — PAGE 5

OX

No, after me.

HARE

After me.

TIGER

No, actually after me.

GOAT

No, me.

DOG

No, name it after me.

NARRATOR

The gods grew so weary of the quarrelling that they decided to stop the argument once and for all.

1ST GOD

(**Off stage**) This is how we will decide; there will be a race across the great river. We will name the coming year after whichever of you wins.

China — PAGE 6

NARRATOR

Now this seemed a good idea. The animals were extremely pleased with it, for each was certain that he was going to win.
And so with much splashing and gurgling and snorting, the great race began.
(**Animals begin to swim across the river**) Ox was strong. Easily he swam far ahead of all the others.
(**Ox moves in front of other swimmers**) Rat was not so strong. But on the other hand, he was very, very cunning. As fast as he could, he paddled until he reached ox's tail. He grasped it firmly and pulled himself up on to the broad, solid back. (**Rat mimes actions to these words**) Ox felt the tickle.

OX

It must be water lapping on my back.

NARRATOR

Ox swam on, thinking only of how he would be the winner of this very important race. But as he reached the other bank of the river, Rat leapt right over his head and landed, in front of him, on dry land.
(**Rat mimes the actions**)

NARRATOR

Ox could only stare. He was so shocked he could think of nothing to say.

China — PAGE 7

2ND GOD

(Off stage) You were strong and fast Ox, but Rat was clever, so he reached this side of the river first. We will give his name to the New Year. It will be the Year of the Rat. However as you were second, the next year will have your name, Ox, the Year of the Ox.

NARRATOR

As each animal finished the race, the gods named a year after it. (Animals climb up river bank as they are named)

3RD GOD

(Off stage) Tiger, third. Hare, fourth. Dragon, fifth. Snake, sixth. Horse, seventh. Goat, eighth. Monkey, ninth. Cockerel, tenth. Dog, eleventh. And last of all, Pig, twelfth.

NARRATOR

So the first twelve years got their names, and after every twelve years the list of names starts again, with the Year of the Rat, then the Year of the Ox, and then each of the others, in exactly the same order as the animals finished that race so long ago, watched in amusement by the gods. That is how this year came to be known as the Year of the . . .

All exit, Chinese Narrator enters

China — PAGE 8

CHINESE NARRATOR

Very interesting. Let us now look at education in China. Schools there begin their day in a very different way to schools in England. On Monday morning, in place of the first lesson, the whole school gathers in the playground for morning assembly. Speeches and music are played over a loudspeaker and the Chinese flag is raised. The children then go into school for their lessons. (Approximately twelve children enter and sit down) When the teacher hears the first bell he or she will stand at the class-room door and look inside (Teacher enters and mimes actions to narrator's words) to see if anyone is absent or any pupil is talking.

1ST PUPIL

Stand up class. (Class stand)

TEACHER

Good morning children.

PUPILS

Good morning teacher.

TEACHER

(Bows to pupils) Sit down.

China — PAGE 9

CHINESE NARRATOR

The teacher bows to the children to show his or her respect and affection for them. Before the 1949 revolution, four out of five Chinese children could neither read nor write. With the aim of bringing education to everybody, schools were set up throughout the country. Today nearly all children attend primary school between the ages of seven and eleven; and many of them complete at least two years of secondary education. The main subjects taught are Chinese language and literature, mathematics and physics, and a foreign language which is often English. Physical exercise is also an important part of the timetable. At mid-morning, lessons stop for everyone to take part in ten minutes of exercise to music. **(Children stand and exercise to Chinese music)**

TEACHER

We will continue this morning's lessons with some interesting facts about our own country.

CHINESE NARRATOR

Very interesting.

TEACHER

I am going to ask you some questions. Which is China's longest river?

China — PAGE 10

1ST PUPIL

The Yangtze. It is 5520 kilometres long.

TEACHER

Correct. Why was the Great Wall of China built?

2ND PUPIL

It was built to keep out the Mongol invaders. It is over 6000 kilometres in length and has an average height of 8 metres.

TEACHER

What is the most common form of transport in China?

3RD PUPIL

The bicycle. Almost everyone in China has a bicycle and uses it. Two-wheeled traffic jams are very common in our cities.

TEACHER

Correct. Class is now dismissed.

All the class stand and mime actions of riding a bicycle to the "PUSHBIKE SONG" as sung by The Mixtures

All exit. Enter Narrator

China — PAGE 11

NARRATOR

When lessons finish, children can play their own games or take part in an activity such as kite flying. Kites have been made in China for over 2000 years. They are made of silk and paper, both invented in China, and of bamboo which grows there.

Children enter with a variety of kites and all children sing

"LET'S GO FLY A KITE" from Mary Poppins

All exit

PRAYER

Thank you God that we don't just belong to our own families.
Help us to realise that we all belong to your family, the family of man.
Please look after all our brothers and sisters throughout the world.
Especially care for those who are sick or hungry.
Help us to treat others as we would like them to treat us.

AMEN

China — PAGE 12

NARRATOR

The Chinese love celebrations and hold many public festivals. The main ones apart from the Chinese New Year are the Moon Festival in late September and the Dragon Boat Festival in May or June. As in Britain, China has many different religions and beliefs such as Buddhism, Confucianism and Taoism and certain religious practices are part of China's public festivals. Each festival starts with a religious ceremony of lighting joss-sticks in a special incense-filled bowl placed in front of the god of that particular festival. The Chinese offer meat, nuts, fruit and cakes, and sometimes special paper money, and families gather round to pray.

NARRATOR

No Chinese festival celebrations would be complete without a dragon. Traditionally the Chinese hold it sacred and believe that it has a supernatural power which enables it to change colour or make itself visible or invisible. The dragon brings good luck and power. It is often shown as pursuing a great pearl. Many people believe that the dragon represents China and the pearl represents wisdom.

Dragon enters to the music of a range of percussion instruments e.g. cymbals, tambourines, gongs etc.

All children sing

"PUFF THE MAGIC DRAGON" (NSC)

Light

PAGE 1

ATTAINMENT TARGETS
SCIENCE: AT15 Using light and electromagnetic radiation: Levels 1, 3a, 4, 5.
ENGLISH: AT1 Speaking and listening: Levels 1, 2a, 2d, 2e, 4, 5d, 6b.
AT2 Reading: Levels 3a, 4a.

CHARACTERS

Sun
Light
Moon
Ahab
Elijah
Star
Fire
Candle
Noah
Noah's family
Up to 10 Narrators
Crowd of onlookers
Prophets of Baal
Israelites
Chorus and Spectrum
Prayer Leader

NARRATOR

In the beginning, when God made Heaven and Earth, the Earth was without form and void, with darkness over the face of the abyss, and a mighty wind that swept over the surface of the waters.

NARRATOR

God said: "Let there be light" and there was light and God saw that the light was good, and He separated light from darkness. He called the light "day" and the darkness "night". When God sent His Son to the world, Jesus said, "I am the Light of the World". He also said to his followers, "You are like light for the whole world. A city built on a hill cannot be hidden. No one lights a lamp and puts it under a bowl; instead he puts it on the lampstand, where it gives light for everyone in the house. In the same way your light must shine before people, so that they will see the good things you do and praise your Father in Heaven."

Light

PAGE 2

Children sing

"JESUS WANTS ME FOR A SUNBEAM" (LGBH)

Enter Sun, Light and Moon

SUN

Light is a form of energy and has phenomenal power. It comes to us from a very bright star called the Sun which is an incredible mass of fire suspended in space. The huge flames give off light which travels through outer space at an amazing speed. It moves at 300 million metres per second! When rays of light leave the Sun they take eight minutes to reach the earth.

LIGHT

I am light. I can't see round corners because I only travel in straight lines. However, I can bounce off surfaces, rather like a ball bounces off a wall. This is called "reflection". Mirrors reflect my light, so does white paper. You see the words on a page only because light from a lamp or from the Sun is reflected off the page into your eyes.

MOON

In 1666, Isaac Newton was the first to discover that sunlight is a mixture of light in all different colours in certain proportions.

Light   PAGE 3

SUN

We call this the spectrum. These are the colours we all see when sunlight shines through raindrops making a rainbow.

Moon:	Red
Sun:	Orange
Moon:	Yellow
Sun:	Green
Moon:	Blue
Sun:	Indigo
Moon:	Violet

Children walk on with rainbow coloured sheets of paper and make a rainbow.

Children sing

"SING A RAINBOW" (AP)

Exit Sun, Light and Moon

Enter Narrator, Noah and his family carrying toy animals

NARRATOR

God promised us long ago by means of a rainbow that He would not destroy the earth.

Light   PAGE 4

NOAH

God has told me that He is very angry because the people are destroying the beautiful Earth that He made. He is going to send a great flood to punish the people. He has told me to make a huge boat out of gopher wood. It has to measure 300 cubits long, 30 cubits high and 50 cubits wide. It must have three storeys to hold all my family and two of every animal.

Noah and his family hammer and saw as if to build a boat

NOAH

I name this ship "Ark".

Children sing

"THE ANIMALS WENT IN TWO BY TWO" (AP)

Noah and his family enter the Ark

ONLOOKER

It's only a shower. Umbrellas are easier than building an ark.

As many onlookers as possible open multi-coloured umbrellas

Light — PAGE 5

NARRATOR

But as the rain went on, the water covered the roads and the fields and the houses. **(Umbrellas come down)** At last there was nothing left to be seen in the whole world, but the Ark, sailing all alone in a world of water. After forty days and nights the rain stopped and Noah sent a dove out to look for land but she couldn't find any. A week later he sent the dove out again and this time she came back with a leaf from an olive tree in her beak. Noah knew they would soon see dry land again.

NOAH

(Points) Look, there is Mount Ararat, we are saved.

NARRATOR

Noah and his family wondered if there would be another flood but God spoke to Noah and told him that He would never send a flood to destroy the Earth again. As a token of His promise, God put a rainbow in the sky.

All exit. Enter 2 Narrators

Light — PAGE 6

NARRATOR

Listen to this definition. . .do you recognise lightning? An electrical discharge between two rainclouds in the sky (called sheet lightning) or between a raincloud and the Earth (called fork lightning). This "jump" is accompanied by a noise, called thunder. **(Sound of thunder)**

NARRATOR

When Ahab **(enter Ahab)** became King of Israel he married Jezebel, the daughter of the King of Sidon. He turned away from Israel's God and worshipped her god Baal.
Elijah, **(enter Elijah)** a prophet, was so upset by this that he said that there would be a drought across all the land until Ahab turned back to God. After three years God told Elijah to show himself to King Ahab.

AHAB

What are you doing here? You are a trouble maker.

ELIJAH

It is not I that have caused the drought but you in turning away from God and His commandments. Summon all the prophets of Baal and all Israel to watch what happens. We will meet on Mount Carmel.

Enter the prophets of Baal and the Israelites

Light

PAGE 7

NARRATOR

All the prophets of Baal and the people of Israel met on Mount Carmel at King Ahab's command.

ELIJAH

How long will you worship this false God called Baal? Come, stop sitting on the fence. You have to decide which is the true God.
I am the only true prophet of the Lord. There are 450 priests of Baal. We shall have a contest to see who is the one true God. Choose two bulls for sacrifice. The prophets of Baal may pick one, cut it up and lay it on the altar to Baal without setting fire to it. I will prepare the other one and lay it on the altar to God without setting fire to it. We will call upon our Gods by name and the one that sets fire to the altar will be the one true God.

NARRATOR

The prophets of Baal agreed to this plan. They prepared their bull and began to call upon Baal to send fire by lightning to burn their sacrifice. All day the 450 prophets of Baal ranted and raved and danced wildly around the altar.

Children dance to "O FORTUNA" (opening and ending of) CARL ORFF'S "CARMINA BURANA"

Light

PAGE 8

NARRATOR

Elijah mocked them.

ELIJAH

Call louder, perhaps he's nodded off or gone on a long journey.

NARRATOR

Eventually the prophets of Baal sank down exhausted and defeated.

ELIJAH

Now it's my turn.
You people, fill four buckets of water and pour it on to the wood of the altar and the sacrifice.
(Water is poured on)
Now do it again   **(More water)**
Now again   **(Even more water)**
See–everything is soaked. If my God can burn this by sending fire in the form of lightning, then you will have to admit He is the one true God.
Oh Lord God–show Yourself and accept this sacrifice.
(Thunder and lightning. A drum beats)

NARRATOR

The lightning set fire to the altar and burned everything in sight.

Light — PAGE 9

All cast bow down and cry
> The Lord is God, the Lord is God.

ELIJAH
> Seize the prophets of Baal. Do not let any escape. All must be slaughtered.

NARRATOR
> All the priests of Baal were taken away and slaughtered. God then ended the years of drought and Israel returned once more to God.

All exit. Enter Star, Sun and Moon

MOON
> **(Turning to the Sun)** You are the source of all light for the planet Earth even though you are so far away.

SUN
> Yes, without me, even though I am 149 million kilometres from Earth your planet would be a very dark cold place. Men have worshipped me. **(Turning to the moon)** Your light is only a reflection of mine.

MOON
> I am 384,400 kilometres away from the Earth and I reflect a gentle light back to the Earth. Men have worshipped me as a silver goddess.

Light — PAGE 10

STAR
> I am a luminous cloud of gas and though the Sun is also a star, most stars are so far away from Earth that they look like pinpricks of light in the night sky.

Children sing

"GOOD MORNING STARSHINE" from "Hair"

Audience can be encouraged to clap during the chorus

Enter Fire, Candle and Narrator

FIRE
> I give both warmth and light. Without me, Earth would be a chilly place for men to live. I am used for heating and cooking. At one time, early man used to keep wild animals at bay with firelight.

CANDLE
> Candles and oil lamps were once the chief form of artificial light. Accurately-made candles which could burn at a steady rate were measured along their length and used as a type of clock. Candles were made of paraffin wax or animal fat with a central wick of string.

NARRATOR
> February the second is Candlemas Day. On this day, people used to bring candles to the church to be blessed, and then carried them in procession, in thankfulness for the gift of light.

Light

PAGE 11

NARRATOR

The Hindu "Festival of Lights" is called Diwali. It is the celebration of the Indian New Year in October or November. At this time, lamps or candles are placed in every window. This is so that Lakshmi, the Goddess of Prosperity can visit homes which are brightly lit and ensure their good fortune in the coming year.

NARRATOR

The Jewish "Festival of Light" is called Hanukkah and celebrates the Jews regaining their freedom to worship in the Temple of Jerusalem. The festival lasts for eight days. Each evening, a candle is lit in an eight-branched candlestick.

NARRATOR

Today the use of light is very sophisticated. We could not manage without it. Just try to imagine not being able to flick on a switch for instant light. Think of a lighthouse and the help it gives to sailors. Think of an airport and the hundreds of landing lights. Just think of a disco without lots of coloured lights.

Suggested hymn "COLOURS OF DAY" (TTS)

Light

PAGE 12

PRAYER

Thank You God for light, which allows us to see where we are going and what we are doing. We remember too that light has long been associated with good understanding and knowledge, and for this reason many schools have a torch as part of their school emblem.
As the light dawns in the East, we thank You for the new dawns in various parts of the world where freedom and happiness are now more possible.

AMEN

Amazing Grace

PAGE 1

ATTAINMENT TARGETS
ENGLISH: AT1 Speaking and Listening: Levels 1, 2a, 2d, 2e, 4, 5d, 6b, 6c.
          AT2 Reading: Levels 3a, 4a.

CHARACTERS
Up to 6 Narrators
Jonah
Captain
1st Sailor
2nd Sailor
3rd Sailor
4th Sailor
4 children tossing pancakes
Rachael
David
Neil
Farmer
Younger Son
Elder Son
3 Servants
Prayer Leader

NARRATOR

If you buy an item for £5 and sell it for £15 you could say you have made a "profit". However, there is another word that sounds the same "p.r.o.p.h.e.t.". In the Bible a prophet was a person who gave people messages from God. Jonah is one of the most renowned prophets and people were prepared to listen to what he had to say. **(Enter Jonah)** One day God told Jonah to go to the City of Nineveh and tell the people to mend their ways because they were behaving very badly.

JONAH

Nineveh! Not Nineveh, anywhere but Nineveh. Please don't send me to Nineveh.

Amazing Grace

PAGE 2

NARRATOR

Nineveh was the sort of city where, if there had been such a force in those days, the police would have patrolled the streets in groups of three or four. The people of Nineveh had turned to crime as a way of life. Jonah, because he was afraid to go to Nineveh, decided to run away to Spain. He boarded a ship at the Port of Joppa but soon after the ship sailed into a violent storm and the sailors were afraid the ship would be smashed to pieces. The crew began to pray to their own gods and then threw most of the cargo, and anything else they could find, into the sea to lighten the ship. While all this was happening Jonah was fast asleep in the ship's hold.

Jonah lies down to sleep

CAPTAIN

Hey you. What do you think you're doing lying down here fast asleep? We are in the middle of a terrible storm. The crew are panic stricken! Get up and start praying to your God for help.

Jonah gets up and is about to exit when four sailors rush on and stop him

1ST SAILOR

Who's to blame for this terrible storm? Someone on board must have done something wrong and this is their punishment.

Amazing Grace — PAGE 3

JONAH
Perhaps it's me. God asked me to do something for Him and I didn't want to do it so I'm running away from Him.

2ND SAILOR
Running away from God? This storm is your punishment from your God then and now we're all going to die because of you.

JONAH
I know this storm is all my fault.

3RD SAILOR
If we punish you maybe the storm will die down and we'll all be saved.

JONAH
If you throw me over the side of the ship I will drown but I'm sure the storm would then calm down.

4TH SAILOR
You must be joking. If your God has done this to you for something you have done wrong, what on earth would He do to us if we threw you overboard?

Amazing Grace — PAGE 4

CAPTAIN
Look the storm's getting worse. We must do something quickly.

1ST SAILOR
It's our only hope.

The first two sailors grab hold of Jonah and take him to the side of the ship. As they are about to throw Jonah overboard the Captain speaks

CAPTAIN
Oh Lord, Jonah is responsible for this storm. Please don't punish us for throwing him into the sea.

Jonah is thrown into the sea

3RD SAILOR
Amazing! The storm is over, the sea is calm. Thank the Lord.

NARRATOR
God made sure that Jonah did not drown. He was swallowed by a large fish and arrived back on land three days later. While Jonah was inside the fish, he prayed to God for help.

Amazing Grace PAGE 5

JONAH'S PRAYER

> I called to You God and You answered me.
> Inside the fish for help I cried.
> You threw me to the bottom of the sea,
> To the mercy of the ceaseless tide.
> I thought You had abandoned me,
> The seaweed wrapped around my head,
> The sea covered me completely
> But You brought me back from the dead.
> You heard me when I prayed to You
> And my earthly life restored.
> Now I will do what You bid me to.
> Salvation comes from the Lord.

NARRATOR

God told Jonah once again to go to the city of Nineveh and give the people his message. This time Jonah did as he was told and he informed the people of Nineveh that because of their wrongdoings their city would be destroyed in forty days. They believed Jonah and stopped behaving so badly. To show how sorry they were, they took off their smart clothes, dressed themselves in sackcloth and put ashes on their heads.

Enter three children dressed in sackcloth with grey powder on their foreheads

Amazing Grace PAGE 6

NARRATOR

Sackcloth was the coarsest and cheapest material available and very uncomfortable to wear. When God saw that the people were sorry for the terrible things they had done, He forgave them and did not punish them after all.
Like the people of Nineveh in the story of Jonah, we can think about our own behaviour and try to improve ourselves.

Suggested hymns: "DEAR LORD AND FATHER OF MANKIND" (SOP)
"GRACIOUS SPIRIT, HOLY GHOST" (SOP)

NARRATOR

The forty days in the Church's calendar, known as Lent, begin with Ash Wednesday. This day got its name from the custom of sprinkling ash on the heads of people. These people wanted to show they were sorry for the things they had done wrong and wanted God's forgiveness. Nowadays rather than wearing sackcloth and ashes, some people give up things they enjoy during Lent. Lent has always been a time for fasting. The day before Ash Wednesday is known as Shrove Tuesday. On Shrove Tuesday, church-going Christians, especially Catholics, go to confession. They go to church to be "shriven" which means to be forgiven. Shrove Tuesday is a day for feasting before the fast. Larders were emptied of all the rich foods people would not be allowed to eat for the next forty days. The forbidden fats were made into pancakes with eggs and milk. It has now become a tradition for people to eat pancakes on this day.

Amazing Grace — PAGE 7

Enter 4 children with frying pans, tossing pancakes and reciting

> Mix a pancake, Stir a pancake, Pop it in the pan.
> Fry the pancake, Toss the pancake, Catch it if you can!

NARRATOR

> Fasting may mean going without food altogether for a certain period of time. It can also mean eating less or not eating certain kinds of food – meat, in particular. When we get up in the morning we "break-fast", as we have not eaten since the day before.
> In most religions, for example Hindu, Muslim, Jewish and Christian, it is customary to fast on certain days of the year.
> Muslims are expected to fast on alternate days, or on one day in three, during the month of Ramadan. They fast from dawn to dusk each day. However, a meal is eaten before dawn and after sunset. Like other religions, they look upon fasting as a form of self-discipline. They also believe that the rich should know how the poor feel when they have to go hungry.
> On the Jewish Day of Atonement, Yom Kippur, the people fast for twenty-four hours. Only the sick and the very young are excused.

Enter Rachael, David and Neil

DAVID

> Tomorrow is Yom Kippur. From sunset tonight we start to fast so we had better have a good meal tonight.

RACHAEL

> Why do we fast on Yom Kippur, David?

Amazing Grace — PAGE 8

DAVID

> Because we have done wrong. We feel that we should give up something we enjoy as a token that we deserve to be punished and that we are sorry.

NEIL

> When we go to the synagogue I hope the Rabbi tells us the story of Jonah. Jonah thought that God should only forgive Jews and he tried to run away when God told him to help non-Jews to find forgiveness. God showed Jonah that He loved everyone and wanted to forgive everyone.

NARRATOR

> Just as God loves every one of us and is always willing to forgive, we should love and forgive one another.

NARRATOR

> "O MAN, FORGIVE THY MORTAL FOE"
> by Alfred Lord Tennyson
>
> O Man, forgive thy mortal foe,
> Nor ever strike him blow for blow.
> For all the souls on earth that live
> To be forgiven must forgive.
> Forgive him seventy times and seven:
> For all the blessed souls in Heaven
> Are both forgivers and forgiven.

Amazing Grace — PAGE 9

PRAYER

O God we are sorry for the wrong things we have done,
For being ungrateful and forgetting to say "Thank you.
Forgive us if we are selfish and unkind.
Help us to be more thoughtful and caring
And to forgive one another as You forgive us.

AMEN.

Children sing

"ALL YOU NEED IS LOVE" as sung by The Beatles.

Enter Narrator, Farmer and his two sons

NARRATOR

There was once a farmer who had a fine farm and two sons whom he dearly loved. His elder son was content to work on the land but his younger son grew bored with the dull life on the farm.

YOUNGER SON

(To his father) Give me my share of the money that is to come to me. I want to travel and make my fortune.

FARMER

I am very sad that you want to leave home but if that is your wish I will not try and stop you. Here is your share of the money. (Gives money to son. Farmer and sons exit)

Amazing Grace — PAGE 10

NARRATOR

The younger son went to a far away country. He made many friends as he had a great deal of money. Soon, he had spent all the money on enjoying himself with his new friends. Then came a famine in the land. He had to get a job with a farmer looking after the pigs and he became so hungry he had to eat the pigs' food.

Enter Younger Son

YOUNGER SON

I was foolish to leave my home where I was well-cared for and well-fed. Even my father's servants have more to eat than I have. I am starving to death. I will go home and tell my father what a terrible mistake I've made and how sorry I am.

Exit Younger Son

NARRATOR

When the Farmer saw his son coming home, (Farmer and Son enter from opposite directions) his heart was filled with love and he ran to welcome him. (Embraces son)

YOUNGER SON

I have behaved badly. I have disappointed you and God. I am not fit to be called your son. Make me one of your hired servants.

Amazing Grace — PAGE 11

FARMER

I forgive you my son. **(Calls out to servants)** Bring out my best robe and put it on him. Prepare the fatted calf and let us eat and be glad, for my son has returned. We will have a feast in celebration. **(Servants begin to prepare feast, music plays)**

Elder son enters and speaks to servant

ELDER SON

What's happening?

SERVANT

Your brother has returned and your father is having a feast for him because he is glad he has come home.

ELDER SON

What! A feast for that lazy good-for-nothing! I'm not going to it! You can go and tell my father.

FARMER

(Comes to talk to son) Please come to the feast. It is your brother who has returned and we must welcome him.

Amazing Grace — PAGE 12

ELDER SON

All these years I've slaved on your farm and you never held a feast for me. As soon as he comes back after wasting all your money you throw a great party for him.

FARMER

My dear son, you are always with me. But your brother is my son too, and I love you both dearly. He is sorry for what he has done and I have forgiven him. I thought that I would never see him again. It was as though he was dead and he is alive again. He was lost and now he is found.

Children sing

"AMAZING GRACE" by Rev. John Newton (TTS)

Mother's Day PAGE 1

ATTAINMENT TARGETS
ENGLISH: AT1 Speaking and Listening: Levels 1, 2, 4d, 5d, 6c.
AT2 Reading: Levels 3a, 4a.

CHARACTERS
Two narrators   2nd Angel   Two Girls
Model Mother   Chorus   Mother
God's voice   Two Boys   Child
1st Angel   Prayer Leader

NARRATOR

The fourth Sunday in Lent is known as Mothering Sunday. This is the day when children give cards and flowers to their mothers to say thank you for all her love, care, guidance and thoughtfulness.

Hundreds of years ago, many people worshipped in small chapels but on Mid Lent Sunday they went to the mother-church of the parish and offered special gifts. This is why Mid Lent Sunday became known as Mothering Sunday. People began to think about their own mothers on this day.

Suggested hymns: "JESUS GOOD ABOVE ALL OTHER" (MHB)
"JESU'S HANDS WERE KIND HANDS" (TTS)
"NOW THANK WE ALL OUR GOD" (MHB)

Enter 2 angels escorting a child who will represent a model of a mother

NARRATOR

When the good Lord was creating mothers, He said:

Mother's Day PAGE 2

GOD'S VOICE

(off stage) She has to be completely washable but not plastic **(Angels wash the model)** and have 180 moving parts **(Angels move parts of model)** all replaceable. She must run on black coffee and leftovers. **(Angel lifts coffee cup to model's lips)** She will have a kiss that can cure anything from a broken leg to a broken heart **(Angels blow a kiss towards the model)** and she must have six pairs of hands.

1ST ANGEL

(Holds up model's hands) Six pairs of hands? No way.

GOD'S VOICE

It's not the hands that are causing me problems. It's the three pairs of eyes that mothers have to have. One pair that see through closed doors when she already knows what the children are doing there. **(While God is speaking the angels are choosing pairs of eyes from a selection and trying them against the model)** One pair in the back of her head that sees what she shouldn't, but what she has to know. And one pair that can look at a child in trouble and say "I understand and I love you" without saying a word.

Mother's Day — PAGE 3

2ND ANGEL

(Pinching the model) It's too soft.

GOD'S VOICE

But tough! You'll never know what she has to endure.

1ST ANGEL

Can she think?

GOD'S VOICE

Yes she can, and reason, and compromise.

2ND ANGEL

(running a finger over the model's cheek) There's a leak.

GOD'S VOICE

Not a leak, it's a tear.

2ND ANGEL

What's it for?

Mother's Day — PAGE 4

GOD'S VOICE

It's for joy, sadness, disappointment, pain, loneliness and pride. I didn't put it there.

Adapted from "MOTHERS ARE MADE IN HEAVEN"

All exit except Mother who comes to life to the music of "MAMMY" by Al Jolson. She begins to busy herself in the kitchen. Enter Narrator

NARRATOR

It is amazing how many different roles a mother plays throughout the day.

MOTHER

(Calls four children by name) It's half past seven. Time to get up.

NARRATOR

(Off stage) Alarm clock.

Mother is keeping busy and 1st child enters

1ST CHILD

What's for breakfast Mum?

Mother's Day — PAGE 5

MOTHER
Toast, cereal, porridge, or you can have a boiled egg if you like.

1ST CHILD
A soft-boiled egg and toast please Mum.

Mum begins to cook

NARRATOR
Cook.

MOTHER
This toaster's not working at all this morning. **(Holds toaster up and examines it)** I wonder if it's the plug?

1ST CHILD
Oh I forgot to tell you Mum, I dropped it last night when I was making some toast for supper.

MOTHER
It could be a loose connection then. Pass me a screwdriver from the drawer over there. **(1st Child passes screwdriver and Mum tightens a loose wire in the plug)** You can have your toast after all, it's working again.

Mother's Day — PAGE 6

NARRATOR
Electrician.

2nd Child enters in pyjamas

MUM
Why aren't you dressed? You'll be late for school.

2ND CHILD
I don't feel very well. I've got a terrible sore throat and my head aches.

MUM
Come here, let's have a look. Open wide.
Mmm **(Feels forehead)** you've certainly got a high temperature.

NARRATOR
Doctor.

MUM
Back to bed for you. Keep warm and I'll bring you a hot drink and some medicine in a few minutes.

NARRATOR
Nurse.

Mother's Day — PAGE 7

3RD CHILD

(From off stage) Mum, I can't find my gym skirt.

MUM

I've washed it and ironed it and it's in your top drawer.

3RD CHILD

I still can't find it Mum.

MUM

Just a minute and I'll come up and find it.

NARRATOR

Laundress.

1st child sits at table, gets out homework, whilst waiting for breakfast

MUM

Here's your egg and toast.

NARRATOR

Waitress.

Mother's Day — PAGE 8

1ST CHILD

Mum, how do you spell "receive"? Is it "ie" or "ei"?

MUM

"I" before "e" except after "c" when the sound rhymes with "e", so it must be "ei".

NARRATOR

Teacher.

1ST CHILD

Thanks Mum. (Packs schoolwork away, begins to eat breakfast)

3rd and 4th child enter quarrelling. 4th child enters waving a letter. 3rd child is trying to grab it back

3RD CHILD

Give me that back!

4TH CHILD

Why? Is it from your boyfriend?

Mother's Day — PAGE 9

3RD CHILD

No, it's from a girl in my class, if you want to know. Give it back.

4th child waves it out of reach

4TH CHILD

Here it is then. Come on then, come and get it. **(Still waving it out of reach)**

MUM

Hand it over. **(Takes it from child)**

NARRATOR

Referee.

MUM

(Turns to 3rd child) Here it's yours, it's addressed to you. **(Gives it to 3rd child)**

NARRATOR

Judge.

4TH CHILD

Mum, can I have an advance on my pocket money?

Mother's Day — PAGE 10

MUM

Why? What do you want it for?

4TH CHILD

It's Dad's birthday tomorrow and I haven't quite got enough to buy his present.

MUM

Here you are. **(Hands out money)**

NARRATOR

Banker.

4TH CHILD

(Exits shouting) Bye Mum.

MUM

What about your breakfast?

3RD CHILD

He's gone, thank goodness. He's always picking on me Mum. It's not fair. He calls me names and teases me all the time.

Mother's Day — PAGE 11

MUM

I've told you before. If you want my advice, you'll just ignore him and he'll soon stop.

NARRATOR

Agony Aunt.

MUM

Come on, you'll be late for school. Have you got everything?

2ND CHILD

Yes, Mum.   **(Collects coat and bag)**

3RD CHILD

Mum, I've got gym club after school. Will you pick me up at 5 o'clock, because it will be dark by then?

MUM

Yes, love. I'll be there.

NARRATOR

Taxi driver.

Mother's Day — PAGE 12

All exit. Child and mother enter and mime to the record "NO CHARGE" as sung by Tammy Wynette

PRAYER

Thank You, God, for a mum who loves me enough to ask me where I am going, who I am going with and when I'll be back.

Thank You, God, for a mum who loves me enough to stand over me for two hours while I tidy my bedroom, when it would only have taken her ten minutes.

Thank You, God, for a mum who loves me enough to let me make mistakes so that I can learn to stand on my own two feet.

Thank You, God, for a mum who loves me enough to accept me for what I am rather than what she would like me to be.

AMEN

Children sing

"MOTHER OF MINE" as sung by Neil Reid.

Time

PAGE 1

ATTAINMENT TARGETS
SCIENCE: AT16 The Earth in Space: Levels 3b, 4a.
MATHEMATICS: AT8 Measures: Levels 2c, 3b.
ENGLISH: AT1 Speaking and Listening: Levels 1, 2a, 2d, 2e, 4, 5d, 6b, 6c.
AT2 Reading: Levels 3a, 4a.

CHARACTERS
1–8 Narrators
Sea
Egyptian
Water-clock
Sand-clock
Candle
Roman
Baby
Old Person
Mad Hatter
Alice
Dormouse
March Hare
1–7 children to recite poem
Chorus
Prayer Leader

Narrator enters

NARRATOR

What is time? Is it something we can all reach out and touch, like water? Is it something only our noses can detect, or our tongues – a smell or a taste? Can we see it or hear it? No.
In effect, time is a scale, or a form of measurement – like weight or distance. Weight is measured in grams and kilograms . . . Distance is measured in centimetres and metres . . . Time is measured in seconds, minutes, hours, days, weeks, months, years, centuries and so it goes on.
Using time as a measuring device, we are able to look into the future, or into the past . . .
Think back, way, way, way into the past when nothing walked the land or swam in the seas . . .

Time

PAGE 2

The hands on a clock-face are moved backwards to indicate going back in time

Enter the Sea

SEA

I am the sea. According to the theory of evolution, life began within me. Small plants and sea creatures developed. These things did not know of "time", however "time" was in existence. Day still merged into night, and night into day. Nothing could stop time pushing on and on. Time has always been around, but it was not thought of until much later.

The hands on a clock-face are moved forward as we travel into the future

NARRATOR

The sea creatures crawled out on to the land and began to turn to two legs for support. Ape-like creatures evolved and man in turn evolved from them. Humans were more intelligent than any of the creatures that had existed before them. Through the years, time became more and more important to them. They began to rely less upon hunting, preferring to grow food for themselves so they had to be able to tell when would be the best time to sow seeds or sacrifice animals to their gods. The first measure of time they used was the day, the time between one sunrise and the next. The next measure was the number of days between the appearance of one new moon and the next. This was called a month.

Time — PAGE 3

NARRATOR

Around the time of the Ancient Egyptians the link between time and the Sun was further developed.

The hands on the clock-face move forwards

Enter Egyptian carrying a stick

EGYPTIAN

It first struck me when I was watching the shadow of a stick placed in the ground. The shadow moved as the Sun moved across the sky. I watched this pattern for some days and noticed that the shadow was in the same position for each part of each day.

NARRATOR

From this "shadow clock," the "sundial" was created. **(Holds up sundial made of card)** This is a very simple timekeeping device. By looking at the position of the shadow it is possible to tell what period of the day you are in. However, it has its problems. It requires the Sun to shine, so it was of no use at all during the night or on a cloudy day.
To satisfy man's need for timekeeping, other methods were invented.

Enter Water-clock carrying a calibrated bucket

Time — PAGE 4

WATER-CLOCK

The water-clock was a large bucket filled with water. It had a small hole drilled in the side allowing water to drip out slowly. The inside was "calibrated" by marking a series of lines. When the water level reached a line, it illustrated how much time had passed.

Enter Sand-clock carrying a large sand timer

SAND-CLOCK

The sand-clock was also known as a "sand timer". By turning it upside down, sand began to trickle from one glass container to another. When all the sand had run through, a known period of time would have passed.

Enter Candle carrying a large calibrated candle

CANDLE

Candles had lines drawn around their circumferences. When the candle had burnt down to one of these lines, a known amount of time would have passed.

NARRATOR

As the years went by man's knowledge of "time" increased. Even before the birth of Christ, the Romans had begun to measure time in hours, days, weeks, months and years. They had even developed a calendar.

Time — PAGE 5

The hands on the clock-face move forwards

Enter Roman

ROMAN

We began the kind of calendar which divided the year into twelve months. These months were no longer based on the moon. They were twelve fairly equal periods of time which began in January.

NARRATOR

This is the kind of calendar used in countries where the main religion is Christian. However, people of the Hindu, Sikh, Buddhist, Jewish and Muslim religions use lunar calendars for their religious and festival year. Many of their celebrations take place at the new or full moon. For Muslims all over the world there are five very important times of the day when they must say their daily prayers. Prayer must be said at dawn, just after noon, before sunset, immediately after sunset and during the early part of the night. Before praying a Muslim always washes his face, hands and feet, stands on clean ground or on a prayer mat and faces Mecca.

Time — PAGE 6

NARRATOR

The importance of Muslim prayer is that it must take place at specific times during the day according to the position of the Sun. Telling the time became much more accurate and reliable with the invention of the first mechanical clocks. These were made in the 1300s, using gear wheels to turn "arms" on a clock face. Next came the pendulum which is still used in the grandfather clock.

Children sing

"MY GRANDFATHER'S CLOCK" (TA)

All exit except Narrator

NARRATOR

Like the grandfather clock, early clocks were extremely large. Nowadays they can be extremely small like the watches on your wrists. During the late 1970s, the digital watch became very popular. Today's timepieces are extremely accurate.
So we have finally arrived at the present but what exactly do we mean by "present", "past", and "future?"
When something is happening now it is in the "present".

Time — PAGE 7

Enter baby

BABY

When something has already happened, it is in the "past". You were just like me once!

Enter old person

OLD PERSON

When something will happen later, it is in the "future". One day you will be just like me!

Exit baby and old person

NARRATOR

What does the future hold for us? No one knows, only time will tell. How much time have we left? We seem to spend a great deal of time wishing our lives away. How often have we said "I wish it was the weekend", "I wish it were the summer holidays", "I wish it was Christmas", "I wish . . . ?" The Mad Hatter in Alice in Wonderland had found the secret of moving time on to the time he wanted it to be.

Enter the Mad Hatter from "Alice in Wonderland" singing "I'M LATE, I'M LATE FOR A VERY IMPORTANT DATE" and looking at his large pocket watch. He is setting out a table and 4 chairs for a tea party. At the end of the song March Hare and Dormouse enter. Dormouse sits in between March Hare and Mad Hatter who rest their elbows on him. Alice enters. Mad Hatter is still looking at his watch

Time — PAGE 8

ALICE

(**Looking over Mad Hatter's shoulder**) What a funny watch! It tells the day of the month and doesn't tell what o'clock it is!

MAD HATTER

Why should it? Does your watch tell you what year it is?

ALICE

Of course not but that's because it stays the same year for such a long time together.

MAD HATTER

Which is just the case with mine.

ALICE

I don't quite understand you. (**Sits down at the table**)

MAD HATTER

The dormouse is asleep again. (**Pours a little tea on to its nose**)

Time

PAGE 9

DORMOUSE

(**Shaking its head impatiently without opening its eyes**) Of course, of course; just what I was going to remark myself.

MAD HATTER

Have you guessed the riddle yet? Why is a raven like a writing-desk?

ALICE

No I give up. What's the answer?

MAD HATTER

I haven't the slightest idea.

MARCH HARE

Nor I.

ALICE

I think you might do something better with the time than wasting it asking riddles that have no answers.

MAD HATTER

If you knew Time as well as I do, you wouldn't talk about wasting it. It's him.

Time

PAGE 10

ALICE

I don't know what you mean.

MAD HATTER

Of course you don't! I dare say you never even spoke to Time!

ALICE

Perhaps not but I know I have to beat time when I learn music.

MAD HATTER

Ah! That accounts for it. Now, if you only kept on good terms with him, he'd do almost anything you liked with the clock. For instance, suppose it were nine o'clock in the morning, just time to begin lessons, you'd only have to whisper a hint to Time, and round goes the clock in a twinkling! Half past one, time for dinner!

NARRATOR

The Mad Hatter in Alice in Wonderland was always rushing around. Like him we spend much of our time rushing from one place to another. If we listen closely to the words of the poet, W.H. Davies, we are made aware of the beauties of nature all around us, which we are often too busy to notice.

Time — PAGE 11

1–7 children enter and recite poem

> LEISURE by W. H. Davies
>
> What is this life, if full of care,
> We have no time to stand and stare?
>
> No time to stand beneath the boughs
> And stare as long as sheep and cows;
>
> No time to see, when woods we pass,
> Where squirrels hide their nuts in grass;
>
> No time to see, in broad daylight,
> Streams full of stars, like skies at night;
>
> No time to turn to Beauty's glance,
> And watch her feet, how they can dance;
>
> No time to wait till her mouth can
> Enrich that smile her eyes began?
>
> A poor life this if, full of care,
> We have no time to stand and stare.

Suggested hymns: "FOR THE BEAUTY OF THE EARTH" (MHB)
"LORD OF ALL HOPEFULNESS" (MHB)

All exit

Enter Narrator

NARRATOR

> The Mad Hatter in Alice in Wonderland had a great deal to say about time. The Book of Ecclesiastes in the Bible tells us there is a time for everything. Everything that happens in this world happens at a time God chooses.

Time — PAGE 12

Children sing

"TURN, TURN, TURN" as sung by Peter Seeger (ST)

PRAYER

> Help us God to make good use of the time You have given us,
> That we may set aside some time to do our own work and also to help others.
> Help us to make the most of every day of our lives, taking each day as it comes, one day at a time.
>
> AMEN

Children sing

"ONE DAY AT A TIME" as sung by Lena Martell.

The Earth in Space — PAGE 1

ATTAINMENT TARGETS
SCIENCE: AT16 The Earth in Space: Levels 1b, 2, 4, 5a, 6.
ENGLISH AT1 Speaking and listening: Levels 1, 2a, 2d, 2e, 4, 5d, 6b, 6c.
AT2 Reading: Levels 3a, 4a.
TECHNOLOGY: AT1 Identifying needs: Levels 2c, 3b, 4a, 5a, 6c.
AT2 Generating a design: Levels 1, 2a, 3, 4, 5a, 5b, 5c, 5d, 6a, 6c.
AT3 Planning and making: Levels 2a, 2b, 2c, 3, 4b, 4c, 4d, 4e, 5.
AT4 Evaluating: Levels 2a, 3a, 3b, 4a, 4b, 5a, 5b.

CHARACTERS

Dr. Who	Earth	Neptune	Major Tom
Sun	Mars	Pluto	Narrator
Moon	Jupiter	Shooting star	Neil Armstrong
Mercury	Saturn	Teacher	Edwin (Buzz) Aldrin
Venus	Uranus	6 Mission controllers	Aliens

Theme music to Dr. Who. Dr. Who enters rotating round stage

DR. WHO

The beginning, the beginning, the beginning, the beginning. I've come back to the very beginning. Many scientists believe that the Universe began in an enormous explosion called the Big Bang which happened about fifteen million years ago. Clouds of gas thrown out by the Bang became galaxies. Even today all the galaxies are racing apart from each other as a result of this initial explosion. Our galaxy is called "The Milky Way" and the solar system is only a part of this galaxy.

The Sun and nine planets enter. The planets gather closely around the Sun.

The Earth in Space — PAGE 2

Music–"ALSO SPRACH ZARATHUSTRA" by Richard Strauss (from "2001 Space Odyssey"). The planets gradually move away circling round the sun randomly at first then gradually assuming their positions in relation to the sun. They freeze in this position as the music ends

Teacher enters

PLANETS

Good morning Miss/Sir.

TEACHER

Good morning class. Our topic this term is "The Earth in Space."

All children sing

"LET'S GO TO THE PLANETS" from "Blast Off" by Stanier & Parker

Teacher, nine planets, and the Sun remain on the stage. They are joined by the Earth's Moon

TEACHER

Sit down. In 1543, Nicolas Copernicus' perspective proposed a solar system with the celestial sphere, a dominant body with orbital planets. Immense gravitational pull held these in check. Movement occurred in elliptical orbits, a fact fully stated by Kepler in his first law of Planetary Motion. Have you got that class?

The Earth in Space — PAGE 3

PLANETS / CHILDREN

Not really.

TEACHER

Let's try it this way then, the Sun and nine planets are called The Solar System. Stand up everybody. **(The Sun and nine planets stand in a line facing the audience. Moon stands in front of the Earth. Teacher stands behind the Sun)** You are the Sun.

The following section has been written by children as a result of their own research and is given as an example. Children may write and read their own research

SUN

I am a star at the centre of the solar system. The Earth and the other planets spin like tops as they orbit me. I shine on different parts of the Earth's surface as it spins. This gives the Earth day and night. My light is so bright; you should never look directly at me, even when you are wearing sun-glasses because that might cause permanent damage to your eyes.

TEACHER

(Moves along the line and points to each planet in turn) Mercury.

The Earth in Space — PAGE 4

MERCURY

I'm the nearest planet to the Sun and orbit it once every 88 days. I am one of the smallest planets in the Solar System and have no air, and no water. I am very rocky and pinkish in colour.

TEACHER

Venus.

VENUS

I am much brighter than any other planet or star. Because I shine so brightly at dawn and at sunset, many people call me the Morning Star or Evening Star. My year is almost the same as 244 Earth days.

TEACHER

Earth.

EARTH

I am like a ball or sphere spinning through space. I am the third nearest planet to the Sun but I am still 150 million kilometres away from the Sun. It takes me 365 and a quarter days to go round the Sun. Because I am always tilted at the same angle, different parts of me face the Sun directly at different times of the year.

continued...

The Earth in Space — PAGE 5

EARTH

When one part has summer with long warm days, the other part has winter and the days are short. This gives me my seasons. I spin upon my axis once every twenty-four hours.

TEACHER

Moon.

MOON

When you look at me from the Earth, I seem to change my shape. I grow from a thin sliver into a bigger crescent. Then I become a half Moon and eventually a whole full Moon. I slowly shrink back to a half, to a crescent and down to a sliver. The whole process takes about a month and my different shapes are called phases. I do not really change my shape at all. It is just that you see different parts of my lit-up side as I orbit the Earth. I have no light of my own. I just reflect the Sun. I have no air or water and there is no life on me. My days are extremely hot but at night my temperature falls far below that on Earth.

TEACHER

Mars.

The Earth in Space — PAGE 6

MARS

I am often called the Red Planet because I look red in the night sky. I am the third smallest planet. The length of my day is almost the same as that on Earth as I spin on my axis every twenty-four and a half hours.

TEACHER

Jupiter

JUPITER

I am the largest planet in the solar system. I take almost twelve years to orbit the Sun. In the southern part of me, there is an object known as the "Great Red Spot". This is a huge red oval into which the Earth would fit. I am surrounded by many red moons.

TEACHER

Saturn.

SATURN

I am the most beautiful planet in the solar system. I have many moons and three rings surround me. I take twenty-nine and a half Earth years to go round the Sun.

The Earth in Space — PAGE 7

TEACHER

Uranus.

URANUS

I am a cold, green-coloured planet. I don't spin like other planets, I roll rather like a ball. I have got several moons and orbit the Sun in 84 Earth years.

TEACHER

Neptune.

NEPTUNE

I am bigger than Uranus but very like it. It takes me nearly 165 Earth years to orbit the Sun.

TEACHER

Pluto.

PLUTO

I am the smallest, remotest and coldest planet in the solar system. To me the Sun is just a tiny, distant speck of light. I travel more slowly than any other planet, my year lasts as long as 247 years on Earth.

The Earth in Space — PAGE 8

TEACHER

"A LESSON IN ASTRONOMY"

(Children act out this poem)

The solar system puzzled us,
    Miss Jenkins said she thought it would,
And so she gave us each a name
And made it all into a game,
    And then we understood.

Patricia with her golden hair
    All loose and shining was the Sun,
And round her Mercury and Mars,
Venus and all the distant stars
    Stood waiting, every one.

I was the Earth, with little Jim
    Beside me for the Moon so round,
And Saturn had two hoops for rings,
And Mercury a pair of wings,
    And Jupiter was crowned.

Then when Miss Jenkins waved her hand,
    Each slow and stately in her place,
We circled round the Sun until
A comet, that was long-haired Jill,
    Came rushing on through space.

She darted straight into our midst,
    She whirled among us like a flash,
The stars went flying, and the Sun
And laughing, breathless, wild with fun,
    The system went to smash.

Anonymous.

Children's names can be changed to the names of those taking part

The Earth in Space — PAGE 9

TEACHER

Even the best planned lessons go wrong.

Suggested hymns: "ONE MORE STEP ALONG THE WORLD I GO" (TTS)
"HOW GREAT THOU ART" (RMHOL)
"THERE'S A WIDENESS IN GOD'S MERCY" (SOP)

All exit. 6 mission controllers enter carrying a spaceship and position centre front. 3 mission controllers stand on each side of the spaceship

CONTROLLER 1

Many of our teachers and some of our parents could not have studied space travel at school. Man did not start travelling in space until 1961. Now we can fly through space to the moon.

CONTROLLER 2

All aspects of space travel are still very dangerous. Every space launch is the result of many months of detailed planning by a large team of scientists and engineers.

The Earth in Space — PAGE 10

CONTROLLER 3

During the actual spaceflight, a team of men and women at Mission Control are responsible for the success of the entire mission.

CONTROLLER 4

Up in space astronauts have to work very hard to keep themselves and their spacecraft in working order. They carry out various experiments. Always at the back of their minds is the feeling that something could go wrong for they are in an alien world.

**Music begins to play. "MAJOR TOM" as sung by David Bowie. Enter Major Tom and climbs on to spacecraft. Major Tom mimes and acts to the words of the song. The controllers watch.
They become very excited and congratulate each other during the successful launch. Gradually as things begin to go wrong they become increasingly concerned, and are in a state of despair at the end of the sequence**

The Earth in Space — PAGE 11

CONTROLLER 5

> PRAYER
>
> We thank You for space, God.
> We all need space,
> Space to move in,
> Space to work in,
> Space to stand back and appreciate.
> We love the wide open spaces
> And clear starry nights.
> We are fascinated by outer space
> Which stretches further than we can understand.
> We pray for those men and women who boldly go
> Where no man has been before.
> Give them courage and give us interest and gratitude.
>
> AMEN

All exit

Enter Narrator

NARRATOR

> The moon has always fascinated mankind and he developed a yearning to reach and explore its mysterious surface. The first man to step on to the moon was Neil Armstrong in 1969.
> **(Stand to one side)**

Music "WALKING ON THE MOON" as sung by Police. Only the first part of this record need be played.

The Earth in Space — PAGE 12

Neil Armstrong enters as if stepping on to the surface of the moon. Volume of music decreases

NEIL ARMSTRONG

> That's one small step for man, one giant leap for mankind.

Volume of music increases. Neil Armstrong walks as if there is little gravitational pull, stops and hammers an American flag into the ground.

All this action and Neil's first words must be timed to fit into the introduction of the music. When the words of the music begin, Edwin (Buzz) Aldrin enters and moon-walks with Neil Armstrong around the stage.

All exit

NARRATOR

> What of the future? Will we discover life on other planets or will some alien creature discover Earth first?

All children sing

"GOOD LOOKING GUYS" from "Blast Off" by **Stanier & Parker.**

Enter Aliens who dance between the audience and sing

"GOOD LOOKING GUYS"

New Beginnings

PAGE 1

ATTAINMENT TARGETS
ENGLISH:
- AT1 Speaking and listening: Levels 1, 2a, 2d, 2e, 4, 5d, 6b, 6c.
- AT2 Reading: Levels 3a, 4a.
- AT3 Writing: Levels 2a, 2b, 3a, 3b, 3d, 3e, 4a, 4c, 4d, 4e, 5a, 5b, 5d, 5e, 6a, 6b, 6c, 6d.

TECHNOLOGY:
- AT1 Identifying needs and opportunities: Levels 2c, 3b.
- AT2 Generating a design: Levels 1, 2a, 3, 4, 5, 6a, 6c.
- AT3 Planning and making: Levels 1, 2, 3, 4, 5, 6a, 6b, 6c, 6e.
- AT4 Evaluating: Levels 1a, 2a, 3b, 4a, 4b, 5a, 5b, 6a, 6c.

CHARACTERS

Up to 13 Narrators
Children to perform "fire dance"
Child to represent a donkey
Mary
Peter
John
Thomas
Children to perform "Lord of the Dance"
Children to read own writing about Easter eggs
Parade of children in Easter bonnets
Chorus
Prayer Leader

NARRATOR

"WINTER AND SPRING" (Anon)

But a little while ago
All the ground was white with snow;
Trees and shrubs were dry and bare,
Not a sign of life was there;
Now the buds and leaves are seen,
Now the fields are fresh and green,
Pretty birds are on the wing,
With a merry song they sing!
There's new life in everything!
How I love the pleasant spring!

New Beginnings

PAGE 2

NARRATOR

Long ago people used to celebrate the return of spring to the earth as the trees burst into leaf and the birds began to sing. It seemed that the darkness and death of winter had been beaten and new life was springing up everywhere. This was the time for everyone to have the biggest celebration of the year, the Spring Festival. Countries with different religious beliefs also have spring festivals. In China, the spring festival is called Ch'ing Ming meaning "Pure Brightness". The Hindu festival of "Holi" celebrates the spring harvest and it is also a fire festival. Bonfires are built to represent the burning of the last year's rubbish and making a fresh start. It is a time for fun, tricks and dancing and everyone joins in.

Enter children who perform a "fire dance" to Indian sitar music

NARRATOR

In different parts of the world, people gave different names to the gods they believed had brought the world back to life. The Saxon Goddess of spring was called Eostre. Her name later became Easter. With the spread of Christianity across Europe, the great Spring Festival was turned into the most important event in the Christian religion. Easter was no longer a festival of nature being renewed by spring but a time to remember that Jesus died "for the sins of the whole world" and to celebrate his coming back to life three days later.

Suggested Hymn: "ALLELUYA, SING TO JESUS" (TTS)

New Beginnings

PAGE 3

NARRATOR

The Jewish people had their own special spring festival, called Passover. Passover celebrates the way in which God freed the Jews from slavery in Egypt. God told the Israelites to kill a lamb and then smear its blood on their doorposts, so that when the Angel of Death "passed over" the country, he would recognise the sign and spare them. The crucifixion took place at Passover time. People realised that just as a lamb was killed to save the Israelites, so Jesus was sacrificed for the sake of mankind. They called him the Lamb of God.

NARRATOR

"THE LAMB" by William Blake

Little Lamb, who made thee?
Dost thou know who made thee?
Gave thee life, and bid thee feed.
By the stream and o'er the mead;
Gave thee clothing of delight,
Softest clothing woolly bright;
Gave thee such a tender voice,
Making all the vales rejoice?
Little Lamb, who made thee?
Dost thou know who made thee?

New Beginnings

PAGE 4

Little Lamb, I'll tell thee,
Little Lamb, I'll tell thee,
He is called by thy name,
For he calls Himself a Lamb.
He is meek, and He is mild;
He became a little child.
I a child, and thou a lamb,
We are called by His name.
Little Lamb, God bless thee!
Little Lamb, God bless thee!

NARRATOR

In springtime, hundreds of Jewish families journeyed to Jerusalem to celebrate the festival of Passover. One year at Passover time Jesus and his disciples set off for Jerusalem too. He rode into the city on a donkey.

Enter child to represent a donkey who recites the following poem

"THE DONKEY" by G.K. Chesterton

When fishes flew and forests walked
    And figs grew upon thorn,
Some moment when the moon was blood
    Then surely I was born.

With monstrous head and sickening cry
    And ears like errant wings,
The devil's walking parody
    On all four-footed things.

continued...

New Beginnings

PAGE 5

NARRATOR

The tattered outlaw of the earth,
> Of ancient crooked will;
Starve, scourge, deride me: I am dumb,
> I keep my secret still.

Fools! For I also had my hour;
> One far fierce hour and sweet:
There was a shout about my ears,
> And palms before my feet.

Suggested hymns: "GIVE ME JOY IN MY HEART" (MHB)
"RIDE ON, RIDE ON, IN MAJESTY" (TTS)

NARRATOR

The day that Jesus rode into Jerusalem is now known as Palm Sunday because of the palms that the crowds waved as they followed Jesus. The week that follows Palm Sunday is known as Holy Week. This was the week leading up to Jesus' death. Jesus was greatly loved by many ordinary people. However, the religious leaders were very jealous of Him because He was so popular. Jesus was arrested, tried and crucified.

Suggested Hymn: "THERE IS A GREEN HILL FAR AWAY" (MHB)

New Beginnings

PAGE 6

NARRATOR

After His death on the cross on Good Friday, He was laid in a tomb and a stone rolled across the opening. Early on the Sunday morning, Mary Magdalene, with a few more of Jesus' friends, went to visit the tomb. She was amazed to find that the stone had been rolled away and the tomb was empty. Mary ran back to Jesus' disciples to tell them the story.

Enter Mary and three of the disciples, Peter, John and Thomas

MARY

But I tell you, I saw Jesus. And that wasn't the only surprise I got. There was a bright shining creature sitting on the stone that had been rolled away from the tomb. He told us to tell you that Jesus was alive. The others ran away but I was so upset, I stayed a little longer. Someone behind me asked me what was wrong. I thought it was the gardener and asked him what he had done with the body. He said my name. I recognised the voice so I turned round and I saw Jesus. I tell you it was Him and He was alive.

THOMAS

It can't have been Jesus. It must have been the gardener. He must have heard your name when the others were talking to you.

New Beginnings — PAGE 7

MARY

I tell you it was Jesus. I saw Him with my own eyes. He is risen from the dead.

THOMAS

You must have imagined it, Mary. Are you sure you went to the right tomb?

PETER

Of course she went to the right tomb. We went to see for ourselves when we heard that the tomb was empty.

THOMAS

What did you see?

PETER

Well we didn't see Jesus but when we went into the tomb, it was empty. Jesus' body had gone from the shelf. All that was left was the linen cloth which had been wrapped round His body.

JOHN

I soon realised what had happened. The tomb was empty because Jesus was alive.

New Beginnings — PAGE 8

THOMAS

Do you expect me to believe that? Someone has obviously taken the body away and hidden it somewhere.

MARY

I've already told you, when the others left, I saw Jesus and He spoke to me.

PETER

Have you no faith at all, Thomas? He is risen from the dead.

THOMAS

How can you say that Peter when you haven't seen Him for yourself?

PETER

I believe He has risen from the dead. I don't know how, but it's true, Thomas. Jesus is risen from the dead.

All exit

Suggested Hymn: "JESUS CHRIST IS RISEN TODAY (MHB)

New Beginnings — PAGE 9

NARRATOR

"THE WORLD ITSELF KEEPS EASTER DAY" (Anon)

The world itself keeps Easter Day,
    And Easter larks are singing;
And Easter flowers are blooming gay,
    And Easter buds are springing:
        Alleluya, Alleluya:
The Lord of all things lives anew,
And all his works are rising too:
        Hosanna in excelsis.

There stood three Marys by the tomb,
    On Easter morning early;
When day had scarcely chased the gloom,
    And dew was white and pearly:
        Alleluya, Alleluya:
With loving but with erring mind,
They came the Prince of Life to find:
        Hosanna in excelsis.

The world itself keeps Easter Day,
    Saint Joseph's star is beaming;
Saint Alice has her primrose gay,
    Saint George's bells are gleaming:
        Alleluya, Alleluya:
The Lord has risen, as all things tell:
Good Christians, see ye rise as well!
        Hosanna in excelsis.

94

New Beginnings — PAGE 10

NARRATOR

All over the world, Easter Sunday is the most joyful day of the Christian year because it commemorates the day on which Jesus rose from the dead. Pealing bells, singing hymns, colourful flower decorations, eating chocolate eggs, new clothes, feasting and rejoicing are all part of Easter Day celebrations. People have always danced when they have something to celebrate for dancing is a sign that life carries on.
In India they tell the story of Shiva Nataraja, the Lord of the Dance. Shiva Nataraja dances on a demon, a sign that life is more powerful than evil. Around him is a ring of fire, a symbol of the unending cycle of life.

All sing and a group of children dance

"LORD OF THE DANCE" written by Sydney Carter (TTS)

NARRATOR

For thousands of years, people have thought of eggs as a symbol of new life and re-birth because they have seen birds hatching from eggs. The early Christians chose the egg as a symbol of Jesus rising to new life from His dark tomb. Long before the days of Jesus, people used to give each other eggs as presents in spring. Long before the modern chocolate egg had been invented people gave each other "pace" eggs. The word "pace" comes from "paschal" or Passover. These eggs were hard boiled and dyed or painted in fancy colours. In some parts of the country it was the custom for children to go round begging for Easter eggs or other gifts.

New Beginnings PAGE 11

All sing

"PACE EGGING SONG" from "A Musical Calendar of Festivals" by Barbara Cass-Beggs

Enter children with painted eggs. Children can read their own prose or poetry about Easter eggs

NARRATOR

Easter is a time for starting afresh and at one time a new outfit or at least a new hat was considered necessary. Ladies used to stroll up and down in Battersea Park, in London, to show off their new Easter hats. Easter Bonnet parades have been popular for many years.

Enter children who parade in Easter bonnets whilst singing

"EASTER BONNET" from "Easter Parade", music by Irving Berlin

NARRATOR

The celebrations that began at Easter will never end. Jesus' rising from the dead showed that life does not end at death. If people follow the teaching of Jesus, then God will give them new life after death.

New Beginnings PAGE 12

PRAYER

O God, we thank You for all the new life of springtime,
For the new leaves and flowers and the newborn lambs.
Help us to understand the real message of Easter.
May we know how much You love us
Through the death and resurrection of Jesus.
Help us to do only the things that please You
By following the example of Jesus, our living Lord.

AMEN.

Suggested Hymn: "LORD JESUS CHRIST" (TTS)

All Creatures Great and Small

PAGES 1&2

ATTAINMENT TARGETS
SCIENCE: AT2   The variety of life: Levels 1, 2a, 2b, 3b, 5d.
ENGLISH: AT1   Speaking and Listening: Levels 1, 2a, 2d, 2e, 4, 5d, 6b, 6c.
         AT2   Reading: Levels 3a, 4a.

CHARACTERS

Up to 16 Narrators	Children to talk about pets	John
Mini-beasts		Fox's Wife
Birdwoman	Chorus	10 young foxes
Fox	Mother Slipper Slopper	Prayer Leader
Grey Goose		

NARRATOR

The Bible tells us, that during the creation of the universe, God commanded, "Let the earth produce all kinds of animal life: domestic and wild, large and small" – and it was done. So God made them all, and he was pleased with what he saw.

Suggested Hymn: "ALL THINGS BRIGHT AND BEAUTIFUL" (MHB)

NARRATOR

Well over a million different kinds of animal are alive in the world today but since new ones are regularly discovered, nobody knows the exact total. The animal world is divided into two major groups; invertebrates and vertebrates. Invertebrates are animals without backbones. These include creatures such as insects, worms, spiders, and crabs. Vertebrates are animals with backbones and include fish, reptiles, birds and mammals. Tiny insects dominate the animal world. There are more kinds of insect than of all the fish, amphibians, reptiles, birds and mammals put together and many more are yet to be discovered and named.

All children sing

"THE UGLY BUG BALL" by Burl Ives

Children in "mini-beast" costumes act and dance

NARRATOR

From early times, the care of animals has been very important. In the time of Jesus, shepherds and their flocks were still a common sight on the hillsides. Jesus said, "I am the good shepherd; I know my sheep and my sheep know me. . .and I lay down my life for the sheep." The shepherd lived with his flock and he guarded them day and night. He protected the sheep against all wild animals. The shepherd really did come to know each animal and they all knew him.
The sheep followed him wherever he led them because they trusted him.

"THE SHEPHERD" by William Blake

How sweet is the shepherd's sweet lot!
From the morn to the evening he strays;
He shall follow his sheep all the day,
And his tongue shall be filled with praise.

For he hears the lamb's innocent call,
And he hears the ewe's tender reply;
He is watchful while they are in peace,
For they know when their shepherd is nigh.

All Creatures Great and Small

PAGES 3&4

All children sing

"THE LORD'S MY SHEPHERD" by W. Whittingham and F. Rous
(MHB)

NARRATOR

Humans and animals have existed together on the earth for millions of years. Animals have been used by humans for food, clothing, tools, currency, companionship, sport and entertainment. They have been domesticated, hunted, worshipped, trained and traded. Animals share our world, without them our planet could not exist as we know it.
Throughout the world there are many different attitudes towards animals. The Jewish–Christian view sees humans as having supreme power over other animals, although the Bible tells us that we must not be cruel or abuse animals in any way.

NARRATOR

Hindus think that animals such as camels, monkeys, mice, snakes and birds should be treated exactly like one's children. They believe that all forms of life have a soul and therefore have a right to exist. They have a deep reverence for life and many are vegetarians.

NARRATOR

Buddhism teaches its followers to have compassion for animals and believes in the right of other animals to live.

NARRATOR

Islam believes that caring for animals is as charitable as caring for humans and cruelty to animals is forbidden.

NARRATOR

"HURT NO LIVING THING" by Christina Rossetti.

Hurt no living thing;
Ladybird, nor butterfly,
Nor moth with dusty wing,
Nor cricket chirping cheerily,
Nor grasshopper so light of leap,
Nor dancing gnat, nor beetle fat,
Nor harmless worms that creep.

NARRATOR

The Royal Society for the Prevention of Cruelty to Animals is the oldest and one of the largest animal welfare societies in the world. The R.S.P.C.A. inspectors and workers care for all kinds of animals. Sometimes they are called out to rescue animals in danger or distress and they also have homes for lost and unwanted dogs, cats and birds.
The Royal Society for the Protection of Birds cares for birds in many different ways. It manages nature reserves in which birds are protected and looks after birds which have been harmed by pollution or various chemicals. We all enjoy watching and listening to a great variety of birds and we can show our appreciation for the pleasure they give us by feeding them when they are hungry.

All Creatures Great and Small

PAGES 5&6

All children sing

"FEED THE BIRDS" from Mary Poppins

A Birdwoman acts out the story

NARRATOR

Some people keep birds as pets but there are also many other animals which make suitable pets. About 50% of all households in the United Kingdom own a pet. People's favourite pets are dogs, cats and budgerigars. The last estimation of the pet population was:

NARRATOR

Dogs. 6.4 million in 5.1 million homes.

NARRATOR

Cats. 6.2 million in 1.2 million homes.

NARRATOR

Budgies. 1.8 million in 1.2 million homes.

NARRATOR

If you own an animal in Britain, you own it in much the same way as you would a bicycle or a watch. But British law also sees animals as being very different from other things you may own.

You are responsible for any damage your pet does to other people or their property and you are also responsible for making sure your animal doesn't suffer. Human ignorance causes animals the most suffering. Many people buy or are given animals as pets and don't take the trouble to learn how to care for them. Caring for animals means not only making sure they are given the right food and that they are vaccinated; it also means taking the care to choose the right pet.

The children can introduce their different pets and talk about why they chose them and how they care for them

All children sing

"HOW MUCH IS THAT DOGGY IN THE WINDOW?"
More Favourite Children's Songs, **by Rosina Coombe (Cassette)**

NARRATOR

Animals that live in the wild have no one to feed or care for them but themselves. Many animals spend their lives in danger of being caught and eaten by a predator. A predator is an animal that kills other animals for food. An animal that is hunted by another for food is known as the prey. However peaceful things may seem in the animal kingdom, plots are continuously being hatched; the rabbit is stunned by fear, the hovering hawk is eyeing its prey and the fox is planning a raid.

All Creatures Great and Small

PAGES 7&8

The following ballad is recited by Narrators and Chorus

NARRATOR

"BALLAD OF THE FOX" (Anon)
A fox jumped up one winter's night,
(Fox enters and acts to the following narrative)
And begged the moon to give him light,
For he'd many miles to trot that night
Before he reached his den O!
Den O! Den O!
For he'd many miles to trot that night
Before he reached his Den O!

NARRATOR

The first place he came to was a farmer's yard,
Where the ducks and the geese declared it hard
That their nerves should be shaken and their rest
  so marred
By a visit from Mr. Fox O!

CHORUS

Fox O! Fox O!
That their nerves should be shaken and their rest
  so marred
By a visit from Mr. Fox O!

NARRATOR

He took the grey goose by the neck
And swung him right across his back;
The grey goose cried out,

GREY GOOSE

Quack, quack, quack.

NARRATOR

With his legs hanging dangling down O!

CHORUS

Down O! Down O!
The grey goose cried out, Quack, quack, quack,
With his legs dangling down O!

NARRATOR

Old Mother Slipper Slopper jumped out of bed,
And out of the window she popped her head:

MOTHER SLIPPER SLOPPER

Oh! John, John, John, the grey goose is gone,
And the fox is off to his den O!

CHORUS

Den O! Den O!
Oh! John, John, John, the grey goose is gone,
And the fox is off to his den O!

Enter John

All Creatures Great and Small

PAGES **9&10**

NARRATOR

John ran up to the top of the hill,
And blew his whistle loud and shrill;
(John blows whistle and exits with wife)
Said the fox,

FOX

That is very pretty music, still–
I'd rather be in my den O!

CHORUS

Den O! Den O!
Said the fox, that is very pretty music, still–
I'd rather be in my den O!

NARRATOR

The fox went back to his hungry den,
(Enter 10 little foxes and the fox's wife)
And his dear little foxes, eight, nine, ten;
Quoth they,

10 FOXES

Good daddy, you must go there again,
If you bring such cheer from the farm O!

CHORUS

Farm O! Farm O!
Quoth they, Good daddy, you must go there again,
If you bring such cheer from the farm O!

NARRATOR

The fox and his wife without any strife,
Said they never ate a better goose in all their life;
They did very well without fork or knife,
And the little ones picked the bones O!

CHORUS

Bones O! Bones O!
They did very well without fork or knife
And the little ones picked the bones O!

All exit

All Creatures Great and Small

PAGES 11&12

NARRATOR

Most animals have evolved some form of defence against their enemies during the many millions of years they have been under attack. However, it takes them a long time to adapt to a new danger. Humans started hunting animals about half a million years ago and many animals have almost been wiped out, or have actually become extinct, because they have no defence against us. Creatures such as the rhinoceros, the elephant and the whale are under threat because of hunting and poaching.

At last we are beginning to understand the need to protect animals against ourselves.

In his poem "The Ancient Mariner",
  Coleridge tells us . . .

"He prayeth best who loveth best
All things both great and small;
For the dear God who loveth us,
He made and loveth all."

PRAYER

We thank You, O God for those animals which we can keep as pets
And for all the enjoyment they give us.
Help us to care for them and show respect and kindness for all creatures great and small.
We pray for the organisations which care for animals and pray that others may follow their example.
Help us to protect rather than destroy so that the creatures we know today can still be enjoyed in the future.

AMEN

All children sing

"BEN" as sung by Michael Jackson

Conservation – An Assembly for May Day

ATTAINMENT TARGETS
SCIENCE: AT5 Human influences on the Earth: Levels 1, 3a, 5a, 6c.
ENGLISH: AT1 Speaking and Listening: Levels 1, 2a, 2d, 2e, 4, 5d, 6b, 6c.
AT2 Reading: Levels 3a, 4a.

CHARACTERS

Up to 2 Narrators	Grandmother	2nd Boy
1st Singer	Chorus	Lifeguard
Mother	1st Girl	4 Placard Carriers
Father	2nd Girl	3 Bucket Carriers
Son	1st Boy	Prayer Leader
Daughter		

NARRATOR

(Shouting) Mayday! Mayday! Mayday! (To audience) Mayday is the international radio distress signal. May Day is the ancient festival on which we celebrate the life and death of the seasons of renewed growth and fertility and our gladness in being alive. Today nature is under threat because of pollution and destruction. If we continue to ignore her call for help we are putting the future survival of man at risk.

Enter all class singing the first verse of "CONSERVATION HYMN", sung to the tune of "We Plough the Fields and Scatter"

> We plough the fields and scatter
> The seed to grow the grain,
> But it is fed and watered
> By heavy acid rain.
> We spray with many herbicides
> To kill off all the weeds,
> But have we all forgotten
> Our bread comes from those seeds?

NARRATOR

Hang on a minute, you're in the wrong assembly. That's a harvest hymn. Our assembly is about pollution not harvest.

1ST SINGER

We know what this assembly is about. If you'd just listen and give us a chance to sing the rest of the hymn, you'd find out that we were in exactly the right assembly. Listen very closely to the words.

NARRATOR

All right then, but it had better be good.

Children sing "CONSERVATION HYMN" from the beginning First verse as before.

> *Chorus* All good gifts around us, Are sent from heaven above
> So help us Lord, Oh help us Lord,
> To treat Your world with love.
>
> Aerosols and fridges
> Are used in many homes,
> Their gases such as C.F.C.s
> Are cracking our ozone.
> The hole is getting bigger,
> Our world will not be safe.
> There'll be no more protection
> From ultraviolet rays.

Conservation – An Assembly for May Day

Chorus

We kill wildlife in forests,
Drop sludge in the North Sea,
Pollute our lovely beaches,
And kill off every tree.
Some people try to stop it,
But most – they do not care.
Some beaches are so filthy,
Not many still go there.

Chorus

We all seem so contented
Despite the fume-filled air,
But people do not realise
Their health it will impair.
By throwing litter all around
They will pollute our earth,
The earth does not belong to man
But man belongs to earth.

Chorus

NARRATOR

(**Talking to the singers**) That's convinced me! Now how do we convince them? (**pointing to audience**)

1ST SINGER

Let's show them what's happening to their Earth.

All exit

Sound of birds singing

Enter Mother, Father, Son, Daughter and Grandmother. They prepare a site for a picnic next to a large sign saying "PLEASE TAKE YOUR LITTER HOME WITH YOU. POLLUTION OUT."

MOTHER

There's nothing I like better than a picnic in the countryside on a hot summer's day.

FATHER

Yes, it's great to get away and relax after a hard week in the office.

GRANDMOTHER

It's so peaceful here.

MOTHER

Yes it is. Even the children are behaving themselves.

SON

Mummy can we go and explore?

MOTHER

Yes, okay, but don't go too far away. Keep an eye on each other and don't wander off.

The children walk over to the sign

Conservation – An Assembly for May Day

DAUGHTER

I wonder what this sign says. **(Tries to read it)** Please tak, tak . . .

SON

Move out of the way. Let me read it, I'm the best reader in my class. **(Reads sign)** Please take your litter home with you. Pollution out.

DAUGHTER

Okay then if you're so clever, what's pollution?

SON

Don't you even know that? It's that thing they've been talking about, everybody's talking about, it's on the television, on the radio, in the newspapers, the teachers talk about it, now we're talking about it. So now you know.

Children return to the picnic

DAUGHTER

Granny, oh Granny, what's this pollution that everyone's talking about?

GRANDMOTHER

Pollution's the mess that the country is in, that we'd all be far better without. It's factories belching their fumes in the air, and the beaches all covered with tar. Now throw all those sweet papers into the bushes before we get back in the car. **(Gives daughter a handful of sweet papers which she throws into the hedge)**

DAUGHTER

Daddy, oh Daddy, who makes pollution and why don't they stop if it's bad?

FATHER

'Cos people like that just don't think about others, they don't think at all, I might add. They spray all the crops and they poison the flowers, and wipe out the birds and the bees. Now there's a good place we could dump that old mattress, right out of sight in the trees.

DAUGHTER

Mummy, oh Mummy, what's going to happen if all the pollution goes on?

MOTHER

Well, the world will end up like a second-hand junk-yard, with all of its treasures quite gone.

Conservation – An Assembly for May Day

PAGES 7&8

The fields will be littered with plastics and tins, streams will be covered with scum and foam. Now throw those pop bottles over the hedge, save us from carting them home. **(Gives daughter two pop bottles)**

DAUGHTER

But Mummy, oh Mummy, if I throw the bottles, won't that be polluting the wood?

MOTHER

Nonsense! That isn't the same thing at all. You just shut up and and be good. If you're going to start getting silly ideas, I'm taking you home right away, 'cos pollution is something that other folk do. We're just enjoying our day out.

All exit, daughter throwing bottles over the hedge on her way out

Adapted from "MUMMY, OH MUMMY" Anon

Music plays "ON THE BEACH" as sung by Cliff Richard

4 children are playing on the beach with a beachball. There is a lifeguard sitting on the top of a step-ladder. If possible, the sea needs to be represented in some way, perhaps a blue sheet

1ST GIRL

Isn't it fantastic, a whole day to play on the beach. No lessons and no one telling us what to do.

1ST BOY

Look, there isn't a cloud in the sky. It's really hot. I'm going to get a brilliant suntan.

2ND GIRL

Remember what Mum said. Don't forget to put your suntan cream on. You know how badly you burn.

1ST BOY

Oh all right. **(Rubs cream on)**

2ND GIRL

Shall we go for a paddle or even a swim?

1ST GIRL

Yes. Why not? We're all good swimmers. It's safe to swim here, besides there's a lifeguard over there. **(Points to lifeguard)**

2ND GIRL

Let's go for a splash. **(Puts feet in the sea, jumps back)** Oh, it's freezing.

105

Conservation – An Assembly for May Day

PAGES 9 & 10

1ST GIRL

(**Runs to the water**) Watch me! Brrr! I see what you mean.

LIFEGUARD

(**Blows whistle**) Health warning to all swimmers. (**Child enters, carrying a placard saying, "5,000,000 TONNES OF INDUSTRIAL WASTE"**) Did you know that every year Britian dumps 5 million tonnes of solid industrial waste into the North Sea? (**One child enters and tips a bucketful of scrap-paper into the sea**)

ALL CHILDREN

Ugh!

1ST BOY

Oh come on, the North Sea is massive. What does a few million tonnes of industrial waste matter?

LIFEGUARD

Ah, but did you know (**Child enters, carrying a placard saying "26,000 TONNES OF OIL". Another child enters and tips a bucketful of black scrap-paper into the sea**) that every year the oil rigs pour out 26 thousand tonnes of oil into the North Sea, not to mention the nuclear waste that is also dumped into the sea.

(**Child enters, carrying placard saying, "NUCLEAR WASTE"**)

2ND GIRL

That's definitely it! I'm not swimming in a sewer.

1ST GIRL

Neither am I.

1ST BOY

I thought we were going to have a fun day out at the seaside. It's not going to be much fun if we can't go in the sea.

2ND GIRL

It's just not fair. I didn't realise that so much horrible waste was dumped in the sea. Mum says it's wrong to drop a sweet paper on the floor and yet our country doesn't seem to mind dumping millions of tonnes of sewage into the sea.

1ST BOY

I feel sorry for all the fish and the other sea creatures. We're complaining because it's spoilt our daytrip but it's their home. It's about time this dumping stopped.

All the signs are turned round. They now read "BEACH POLLUTED. NO BATHING."

Conservation – An Assembly for May Day

2ND BOY

I agree. It's spoilt my day. I was really looking forward to a paddle but you won't catch me going in there. **(Points to the sea)**

All exit

The following statements are a result of children's research. These can be added to or substituted by research into current pollution problems. Enter Narrators who say

Do you realise that at the present rate of destruction by the year 2025, we may have destroyed all the Earth's rain forests?

Do you realise that about 12% of the rain forests have already been destroyed and 250,000 square kilometres are lost each year?

Do you realise that half the world's species of plants and animals depend on the rain forests for their survival?

Do you realise that over the past 300 years, 300 species of animals have disappeared from the face of the earth?

Do you realise that rain more acidic than vinegar has fallen in parts of Britain?

Do you realise that acid rain caused by pollution from Britain has fallen on Scandinavia and killed trees and fish stocks?

Do you realise that every ocean in the world now has some measurable pollution?

Do you realise that sewage and atomic waste are two of the deadly products that are tipped into the sea?

Do you realise that unless we change our selfish ways, the world will not be fit to live in?

Suggested Hymns: "THINK OF A WORLD" (TTS)
"ALL THINGS BRIGHT AND BEAUTIFUL" (MHB)
"MORNING HAS BROKEN" (MHB)

NARRATOR

It is very difficult to imagine what the world would be like if many of its beauties were destroyed. This destruction does not have to happen. Each of us has the power to slow down the pollution of our Earth.

PRAYER

Mayday, Mayday,
O Lord, Your beautiful world is being spoilt.
Help us to look after and enjoy it, now and in the
 years to come.
Help us to realise the importance of caring for the
 forests, the rivers and oceans,
And all the animals, birds, insects and other creatures
 that live in them.
Give us the knowledge and the understanding to
 preserve the world which You created
That future generations may enjoy all that You
 entrusted to us.

AMEN

Children sing

"WHAT A WONDERFUL WORLD" as sung by Louis Armstrong

The Other Man's Grass is Always Greener

PAGES 1 & 2

> **ATTAINMENT TARGETS**
> ENGLISH: AT1 Speaking and Listening: Levels 1, 2a, 2d, 2e, 4, 5d, 6b, 6c.
> AT2 Reading: Levels 3a, 4a.

CHARACTERS

Up to 3 Narrators	Hilary's Mother	Doctor
Harry	Hilary's Father	Dog
Hilary	Nurse Broyce	Chorus
Eric	Nurse Smith	Prayer Leader

Children sing

"THE OTHER MAN'S GRASS IS ALWAYS GREENER"
as sung by Petula Clarke

NARRATOR

Perhaps you have heard the saying "the other man's grass is always greener". Often, when we consider other people, we come to the conclusion that they are "well-off", perhaps better off than we are. We say that their "grass is greener". However, appearances can be deceptive as we are about to see.

A play based on "THE WELL-OFF KID"
by Bill Naughton, from
"THE GOALKEEPER'S REVENGE"

SCENE 1

The stage is set with two beds

NARRATOR

Two new patients were admitted to the Children's Ward of the General Hospital that morning. Harry, who is very shabbily dressed, arrives with his brother, Eric. Hilary, who is very well dressed, arrives with his parents. Harry had been in an accident and Hilary was due to have a small operation to change the shape of his ears. **(Harry, who is badly dressed, is carried in on a stretcher and placed on one of the beds. His older brother Eric is with him)**

Enter Nurse Broyce

NURSE BROYCE

Hello. What's your name and what on earth have you been up to?

ERIC

He's called Harry. We were playing football in the street and he had an argument with a car.

HARRY

(sits up) There ain't nothin' wrong with me!

NURSE BROYCE

I'm sure there isn't but they won't take our word. You'll have to let the doctor see you.

ACTIVE ASSEMBLIES FOR THE NATIONAL CURRICULUM — SCHOFIELD & SIMS LTD

The Other Man's Grass is Always Greener

PAGES 3&4

ERIC

    I'd best be off now. **(begins to walk away)**

HARRY

    Don't forget to tell Mum, tell her there ain't a thing wrong with me. Say they just brought me in for a rest.

Exit Eric

Enter doctor

DOCTOR

    (Examining Harry) There won't be much resting for you, young man. These nurses need someone to help serve the food.

HARRY

    I'm willin'.

Hilary walks in with his parents. His father is carrying a pile of toys and books. His mother helps him into the bed next to Harry.

MOTHER

    Bye darling. Be brave. Mummy'll be back soon.

Hilary begins to howl loudly

FATHER

    Don't cry son. We'll soon have you home again.

Father leads mother out. She is crying and doesn't want to leave

Enter Nurse Smith

NURSE SMITH

    (Aside to Nurse Broyce) Those two boys are the same age but they seem as unlike each other as any two kids could be.

While the nurses are talking, Harry is playing with a rabbit's foot and smiling as he looks around. Hilary is lying staring at the ceiling, occasionally wiping his eyes with a handkerchief

NURSE BROYCE

    Well, Hilary, I think we'd better be putting your books and toys away. Would you like something to read before "lights out"?

HILARY

    (Whispers) No thank you Nurse.

NURSE BROYCE

    (Turning to Harry) Now what have you got there, Harry?

HARRY

    It's my rabbit's foot, Nurse. It don't half bring me luck.

The Other Man's Grass is Always Greener

NURSE BROYCE

You'll need it if you keep on playing football in the street.

HARRY

Naughty, wasn't I?

Hilary whimpers

HARRY

(**to Hilary**) Just think of the fun we'll have if they keep us here till Christmas.

HILARY

Christmas! So long!

HARRY

You never know your luck. My brother Eric was in hospital one Christmas–told us all how smashin' it was.

NURSE BROYCE

Have you any brothers, Hilary?

HILARY

No, Nurse, there's only me.

HARRY

I've three brothers...and one sister. 'Course I ain't seen her yet–my sister.

NURSE BROYCE

Oh, (**tucking Harry in**) and how's that Harry?

HARRY

Because she ain't been born yet.

Hilary sits up

HILARY

But you can't know whether you've a sister or not, until she's born.

HARRY

My mum has promised us a sister. She's going to have a baby any day now.

HILARY

But that doesn't follow that it will be a sister. Does it, Nurse?

110

The Other Man's Grass is Always Greener

PAGES 7&8

HARRY

When my mum promises us something, she sees we get it. So I've got three brothers, and a sister to come. Got me?

HILARY

(**Hesitates**) Oh, I see. Uh, good night.

HARRY

Good night, mate. Good night, Nurse.

HILARY

Good night, Nurse.

Lights go out

SCENE 2

NARRATOR

In three days Harry's bruises were out and his scratches were healing. He was ready to go home.

Harry is serving Hilary with drink when Eric arrives to take him home

Enter Eric

ERIC

Mum was sorry she couldn't come, Nurse, so she asked me to thank you for all you'd done. She had a baby last night.

NURSE BROYCE

Well, how nice. Is everybody well?

ERIC

Oh fine. Lovely baby, weighs...

HARRY

What is it? Boy or a girl?

ERIC

Why, it's a boy.

HILARY

What did I tell you Harry? Just because your mother promised you a sister it didn't mean you would have one.

NURSE BROYCE

(**Sympathetically**) Oh what a shame, Harry.

The Other Man's Grass is Always Greener

HARRY

(**Happily**) It don't have to be this time, Hilary. My mum's promised us a sister, she'll see we get one. So now I've got four brothers and a sister to come. (**He shakes hands with Hilary**) I reckon them ears'll look a treat when they take them bandages off, mate. I'll have to come in one day an' have mine done. So long Hilary. Good luck. Goodbye everybody, goodbye.

Nurse Broyce sees Harry off stage and waves goodbye

Nurse Smith enters

NURSE BROYCE

Young Harry just left.

NURSE SMITH

Harry? Was Harry the well-off kid?

NURSE BROYCE

(**Thinks for a moment**) Yes. Harry was well off.

NURSE SMITH

(**Becomes aware of Hilary who is sitting up wiping his eyes**) Hey, Broyce, I thought you said that the well-off kid had left!

NURSE BROYCE

He has. I mean young Harry.

NURSE SMITH

Do you call him well-off?

NURSE BROYCE

Yes I do. He came in here full of cheer and good faith, and he spread them all around the place. Those are things money can't buy. And if young Harry isn't well off, nobody ever was!

All exit

NARRATOR

We often say that some people are "well-off", but just what do we mean by "well-off"? Some may have the latest bicycle, an expensive computer or plenty of pocket money, all things that money can bring. However, no matter how many possessions some people have, they are not necessarily "well-off". There are so many things that money just cannot buy; a cheerful, happy nature, a sense of humour, a willingness to help others and a love of living.

Children sing

"CAN'T BUY ME LOVE" as sung by The Beatles

The Other Man's Grass is Always Greener

PAGES 11&12

NARRATOR

Some people just don't realise when they are well-off. Many religions and cultures use stories about animals to explain human problems. Aesop wrote a story about a dog who wasn't content with what he had. This is what happened to him. A dog was feeling very proud of himself. **(Enter dog with large bone in his mouth. He acts out the story)** He had found a large bone and was carrying it away in his mouth, to eat it in peace somewhere.

He came to a stream and began to cross over a narrow plank to the other side. Halfway across the stream, he paused, panting and looked into the clear, clean water. He jumped as he saw another dog, with a bone in its mouth, looking up from the water. He glared threateningly at the dog in the water and the dog in the water appeared to glare back.

DOG

(Puts bone under paw) If I had that bone, I could eat it now and save mine for later. I know just the place to bury it. Besides, that bone looks bigger and better than mine and it's got more meat on it. **(Growls)**

NARRATOR

The dog in the water appeared to growl back at him.

DOG

So you want a fight, do you? **(Picks up his bone and growls)**

NARRATOR

The dog opened his mouth to grab the second dog's bone and his own bone fell into the stream and was swept away by the current. The dog barked angrily as the dog in the water vanished beneath the ripples. When the surface became smooth again, he was left staring at his own reflection. He felt rather foolish and very hungry when he realised what had happened. The moral of Aesop's story is "Be content with what you have".

PRAYER

We thank You God for the many gifts You have given us,
Gifts that money cannot buy.
Keep us from being envious of those who may seem "well-off".
Make us grateful for what we have and eager to share our happiness with others.

AMEN

Suggested Hymn: "SHOW ME A WAY OF LOVING AND LIVING" written by Harold Clarke (TTS)

Sport for All — PAGE 1

ATTAINMENT TARGETS
ENGLISH: AT1 Speaking and Listening: Levels 1, 2a, 2d, 2e, 4, 5d, 6b, 6c.
AT2 Reading: Levels 3a, 4a.

CHARACTERS

Olympic runner	Eddie Brodsworth	Disappointed child
Up to 9 Narrators	Footballer	Batsman
5 children with Olympic rings	Crowd of football supporters	Bowler
1st runner	Chorus	Fielder
2nd runner		Prayer Leader

Olympic runner enters to the music of "CHARIOTS OF FIRE" by Vangelis

He is carrying the Olympic torch

OLYMPIC RUNNER

The Olympic Games, which are held every four years, are based on the games which the ancient Greeks started at Olympia nearly three thousand years ago. The Olympian Games were held in honour of Zeus, King of the gods, and took place in his temple. The games were part of a religious festival. It was hoped they would bring about peace between the warring tribes and city states of Greece. The Games brought them all together at Olympia, where their desire to fight was used up in running, boxing and jumping. In 1894 the first modern Olympic Games were held, not at Olympia but at Athens.
The Olympic torch was first carried by relays of runners from Olympia in Greece to wherever the games were being held.

Sport for All — PAGE 2

NARRATOR

The most important thing in the modern Olympic Games is not to win but to take part. Today, thanks to the Olympic Movement, athletes from different nations, colours and religious backgrounds are encouraged to come together in peace, to compete in sport.
(Enter 5 children, each carrying an appropriately coloured Olympic ring. They form the sign of the Olympic Games with the rings) Five rings form the sign of the Olympic Games. They symbolise the coming together of athletes from five continents.

Suggested Hymn: "LIFE IS BETTER" by Harold Clarke (TTS)

All exit

NARRATOR

The marathon is the longest running-race in the Olympics. "City" marathons such as the London and New York marathons have become very popular for runners of all ages and abilities. Many disabled people compete in these races and also in a wide range of other sporting events. The main purpose of marathon running is often to raise money for charity. The competitors hope to complete the course if possible and therefore need to begin training well before the event takes place.

1st Runner bursts in

Sport for All — PAGE 3

NARRATOR
Just a minute. Where do you think you're going?

1ST RUNNER
I'm in a race.

NARRATOR
I thought as much when I saw the running gear – shorts, vest, trainers. Is that sort of outfit necessary?

1ST RUNNER
Oh yes, I'll say it is. The lighter your clothes are, the faster you can run and this sort of athletic strip doesn't get in the way either.

NARRATOR
You don't seem to be out of breath to say you're in a race?

1ST RUNNER
That's because I've been training hard for weeks and weeks. Circuit training, weight training, tones up the muscles and gets the heart and lungs in tip top condition.

Sport for All — PAGE 4

NARRATOR
Do you think all that training is going to help you win the race, then?

1ST RUNNER
I hope so. I am determined to cross the finishing line so I'd better get a move on. I can see one or two others catching up on me.

NARRATOR
Yes, you keep going. Best of luck. Hope you make it.

1st Runner jogs off

2nd Runner staggers in

NARRATOR
Are you all right?

2ND RUNNER
Yeah. I think so. . .I'm in a race. . .got to keep going . . .It's no good. . .have to rest . . . **(pant pant)**

NARRATOR
You're never in the same race as the runner who's just been through here are you?

Sport for All — PAGE 5

2ND RUNNER

Yes, there's only one race being run today. Quite a few people overtook me coming up that last steep hill.

NARRATOR

Don't you think it would make it easier if you wore fewer clothes and if you weren't carrying such a heavy bag?

2ND RUNNER

Crumbs no! Want me to catch my death of cold or something? As for my bag, I've got to take it with me, it's full of emergency supplies.

NARRATOR

What do you mean, emergency medical supplies in case you fall and hurt yourself?

2ND RUNNER

No, no chance, emergency food supplies. **(Unpacks bag)** Four ham sandwiches, two packets of crisps, a flask of tea, a flask of coffee and two jam doughnuts, just in case I get hungry on the way.

NARRATOR

Do you do much training before a race like this then?

Sport for All — PAGE 6

2ND RUNNER

Training, no, waste of time if you ask me. What's the point of tiring yourself out every night? I keep up my strength by eating as much as I can.

NARRATOR

Do you think you'll finish the race, then?

2ND RUNNER

Doesn't really bother me either way so long as I'm home in time for my favourite television programme. **(Looks at watch)** Hey, I've only got ten minutes, I'd better be on my way.

NARRATOR

Yes, I think you'd better. You've got a lot of catching up to do.

Second runner exits

NARRATOR

The first competitor had all the necessary equipment to do well. He had trained hard over a long period of time to make sure he was absolutely fit. Most important of all he was determined to do well and had prepared himself thoroughly in order to be successful in the race.

continued . . .

Sport for All

The second competitor had not prepared himself properly. He was wearing unsuitable clothing, had not trained and was therefore unfit. He was carrying far too much unnecessary weight and most importantly he did not care whether he did well or not.

To do anything well we must have a positive attitude and be prepared to work hard like the first competitor.

All children sing

"RUN FOR HOME" as sung by Lindisfarne

NARRATOR

The Bible tells us that Paul wrote to the Church in Corinth. He said that being a Christian was like running in a race:

Many runners take part in a race
Only one of them wins the prize
We crown the winner with a wreath of leaves
Which withers and then dies.
Competitors must prepare thoroughly
And regularly exercise.

So run the race of life to win,
To reach the goal above,
The greatest prize in the race of life
God's everlasting love.

NARRATOR

There are some very successful people in the world of sport but many people can only dream about getting to the top. The very dream of success is exciting, never mind the real thing.

Sport for All

Two children act to the following commentary

It looks like the players are coming out now.
Yes they are.
the crowd erupts,
Screaming for their young hero,
Eddie Brodsworth.
The pitch at the Red Rec
Has undergone a late inspection.
Stones and bricks removed.
He coolly steps up to the centre,
Dressed in his school uniform.
He hears the referee's whistle
And kicks the ball back,
Ready for action.
*. . . . . takes the ball in midfield
***(A famous footballer's name to be inserted)**
And passes straight back to Brodsworth.
He runs towards the defence,
Dribbling brilliantly.
A hard tackle
But Brodsworth stays on the ball.
He splits the defence in half,
Takes one winger, takes another.
Intercepted by the Golden Retriever
But Brodsworth using all his skill
Regains control.
Then with a fantastic scissor kick,
Leaves the goalie standing.
The crowd roars.
Brodsworth has scored a great goal.

Enter a crowd of football supporters who congratulate Eddie

Sport for All — PAGE 9

All children sing

"HE'S FOOTBALL CRAZY" (JH)

NARRATOR

Sport is not just about individual achievement. It also teaches people to work together in teams. To enjoy sport it isn't necessary to be the best. Sport can be a very enjoyable and worthwhile activity for all if everyone is given the opportunity to become involved. However, some people always seem to be left out of the fun or are the very last to be chosen when teams are being picked.

Enter child looking disappointed

DISAPPOINTED CHILD

Why doesn't anyone ever choose me?
Do they know what it's like to be
Always left till the very last?
Just because I can't run fast.

Why doesn't anyone ever choose me?
A more skilful player I'd love to be.
Perhaps my skills I could enhance,
If only they'd give me a sporting chance.

NARRATOR

All sport has winners and losers. Everyone enjoys winning but no one enjoys losing. The way in which we accept success or failure is very important.

Sport for All — PAGE 10

There are "good sports" who can win without being boastful and can lose without sulking. There are also "spoilsports":

Enter group of "spoilsports" including one child with a bat, one child with a ball and a fielder

BATSMAN

It's my bat and I'm not playing if I can't bat first.

BOWLER

Well, it's my ball so I'm bowling.

FIELDER

I'm not fielding again. It's not fair. You always bat first.

BATSMAN

You can bat next. Let's get started. **(Fielder walks sulkily to his position. The first ball is delivered and hits the batsman on the leg)**

BOWLER

Howzat!

FIELDER

OUT! Leg before wicket!

Sport for All — PAGE 11

BATSMAN

No way! It was nowhere near the stumps.

FIELDER

(Tries to take the bat from the batsman) Come on you're out. It's my turn now.

BATSMAN

It's my bat and if I'm out I'm going home and taking my bat with me! **(Walks off with his bat under his arm. The others shout after him)**

ALL

Spoilsport!

NARRATOR

Whatever team game you play – football, cricket, netball, or rounders, the spirit in which you play makes all the difference. Skilled players play unselfishly and everyone enjoys the game.

Sport for All — PAGE 12

PRAYER

Thank you God for the enjoyment and pleasures of sport.
Help us to co-operate with others and keep the rules.
Thank You for the joy of winning
And help us to accept the disappointment of losing,
Help us to remember that the important thing is not to win but to enjoy taking part.
May we love the game above the prize.

AMEN

Sound — PAGE 1

ATTAINMENT TARGETS
SCIENCE: AT14 Sound and Music: Levels 1, 2a, 3, 4, 5, 6a, 6b
ENGLISH   AT1   Speaking and Listening: Levels 1, 2a, 2d, 2e, 4, 5d, 6b, 6c.
              AT2   Reading: Levels 3a, 4a.
TECHNOLOGY: AT1   Identifying needs and opportunities: Levels 2c, 3b, 4a, 5a, 6c.
              AT2   Generating a design: Levels 1, 2a, 3, 4, 5a, 5b, 5c, 5d, 6a, 6c.
              AT3   Planning and making: Levels 2a, 2b, 2c, 3, 4b, 4c, 4d, 4e, 5.
              AT4   Evaluating: Levels 2a, 3a, 3b, 4a, 4b, 5a, 5b.

CHARACTERS

Up to 4 Narrators	Noise Investigator	Doctor
Israelites	Noisy Child	4 Children
Joshua	Patient	Chorus
11 Priests	Prayer Leader	

NARRATOR

Sound can be made in many different ways **(a range of sound effects can be used here, for example, children clapping, shouting, whistling, playing instruments)** but sound is always made by something moving. A sound makes tiny particles in the air bump into each other or vibrate. The vibrations are called sound waves.
(A group of children enter and dance to "GOOD VIBRATIONS" as sung by The Beach Boys. The dance needs to suggest vibrating air molecules making sound waves. This could be achieved through jostling, bumping movements in a wave formation)

continued . . .

120

Sound — PAGE 2

If these vibrations reach our ears, we hear the sound. Sound waves travel through any solid, liquid or gas but not vacuum like space because there is nothing there for the sound to move in.

All exit

NARRATOR

Even in Old Testament times the people seemed to understand enough about sound to use it to their advantage. The story of Joshua and the walls of Jericho is an example of this.

Enter Narrator, and the people of Jericho. People of Jericho hold sheets together to represent the walls of the city, some holding spears

Enter Joshua. Seven priests, each carrying a trumpet, walk in front of four more priests carrying the Ark. The Ark could be a small highly-decorated cardboard box carried on two poles. The rest of the Israelites follow

NARRATOR

When the Israelites reached the land that God had promised them, they found that the gates leading into the city of Jericho were shut. Jericho was heavily defended but God gave Joshua his instructions for capturing the city.

ISRAELITE

How are we going to get inside the city, Joshua? The gates are locked and the walls are huge and heavily guarded.

Sound — PAGE 3

JOSHUA

We will follow God's plan. Four priests will carry God's laws in the Ark of the Covenant and another seven priests blowing trumpets will march in front of it. We will have guards in front of and behind the Covenant Box. **(Israelites get into formation)** We will all march round the city, with trumpets sounding, once a day for six days. **(The Israelites march round Jericho once, blowing the trumpets)**

NARRATOR

And so the marching and the trumpet sounding went on, once a day for six days. The people of Jericho wondered what was happening and felt rather frightened. On the seventh day, Joshua told the people the final part of God's plan.

JOSHUA

Today is the seventh day and we must march round the city seven times. When the priests blow the trumpets you must shout as loud as you can and the walls will fall down.

The Israelites march round Jericho seven times and when the trumpets sound they shout as loud as they can and the walls fall down. All the Israelites cheer and exit, dragging the people of Jericho with them

All children sing

"JOSHUA FOUGHT THE BATTLE OF JERICHO" (A)

Sound — PAGE 4

NARRATOR

The daily marching, the sounding of the trumpets and the final shout, combined to amplify the vibrations. These strong vibrations could have shaken the foundations which may have caused the walls of Jericho to collapse. Not so long ago, soldiers crossing a bridge were ordered to "break step" as otherwise the vibrations resulting from their rhythmic marching could have caused the bridge to sway and possibly break apart.

NARRATOR

When sound waves hit a barrier such as a cliff or the walls of a tunnel, they bounce back and we hear the sound again. This reflected sound is called an echo.

Children sing

"LITTLE SIR ECHO" *Twenty All Time Children's Favourites* – St. Winifred's School Choir – EMI (Cassette)

NARRATOR

Unpleasant sounds are often called noise. Too much noise is not only annoying but dangerous. It is, therefore, important to control noise in the environment. Our investigator has been out and about in this area with his decibel detector.

Enter Investigator with decibel detector

Sound

PAGE 5

NOISE INVESTIGATOR

> **(Holds up decibel detector)**
> A wonderful machine this decibel detector,
> A measurer of noises and an ear protector.
> No noise too loud,
> No noise too low,
> I'll sound them out, away we go.

Walks around with detector

Two children enter whispering just loud enough to hear

Detector pulls investigator towards the noise

NOISE INVESTIGATOR

> What have we found?
> Faint waves of sound.
> 20 decibels on the meter,
> Quite acceptable, not a loud-speaker.

Two children enter having a conversation

Detector pulls investigator towards the noise

NOISE INVESTIGATOR

> A stronger sound,
> More energy I've found,
> 50 decibels on the meter,
> A very clear and audible speaker

One child enters pushing a vacuum cleaner

Detector pulls investigator towards the noise

Sound

PAGE 6

NOISE INVESTIGATOR

> The strongest sound
> So far I've found.
> 70 decibels on the meter,
> A very noisy carpet beater.

One child enters with a large model aircraft to the sound of a jet aircraft taking off

Detector pulls investigator towards the noise

NOISE INVESTIGATOR

> A deafening sound
> As an aircraft leaves the ground.
> 150 decibels, we surrender,
> Protect your hearing with an ear defender.

Investigator puts on ear defenders

NOISE INVESTIGATOR

> Another sound that some people find unpleasant is that of thunder and lightning especially at night. **(Removes ear defenders)** Lightning is a big electrical spark that travels from the clouds to the ground at high speed. The flash can be seen as soon as it happens because light travels so fast, at a speed of 300,000 kilometres in one second. The rumble of thunder follows later, as sound travels much more slowly at a speed of 330 metres in one second. It is illegal to make noise above a certain level. Very loud noises over 120 decibels can cause damage to the ears which receive the sound.

Sound

PAGE 7

Enter child listening to a loud cassette player

NOISE INVESTIGATOR

Turn that down. It's hurting my ears! What a dreadful noise!

Child exits and switches cassette player off

NOISE INVESTIGATOR

(**Holds hands over ears**) Most of us have experienced ear-ache at some time or another and may have needed to visit the Doctor.

Exit

Enter Doctor and Patient

PATIENT

Good morning, Doctor. I've got this terrible pain.

DOCTOR

How often does it come?

PATIENT

I never know when it's going to strike. One minute I'm sitting on my chair. The next minute I'm rolling on the floor. (**Rolls on floor crying with pain**)

Sound

PAGE 8

DOCTOR

Does rolling on the floor get rid of the pain?

PATIENT

No.

DOCTOR

You still haven't told me where the pain is.

PATIENT

Ear.

DOCTOR

Have you got a sore ear?

PATIENT

No I haven't got a saw here. What do you want a saw for? Are you going to cut my ear off?

DOCTOR

Of course not. Can you tell me when the pains in your ear started?

Sound

PAGE 9

PATIENT

It was after I had been camping. It was an earwig.

DOCTOR

How do you know it was an earwig?

PATIENT

My friend saw it crawl in.

DOCTOR

I think the best thing would be for me to try and pull the little fellow out.

PATIENT

Will it hurt?

DOCTOR

Not very much. Please lie on the bed. **(Patient lies on bed)**

PATIENT

Can you see the earwig?

Sound

PAGE 10

DOCTOR

No. All I can see is a bent hairpin. **(Holds up hairpin to audience)**

PATIENT

I tried to get the earwig out with that.

DOCTOR

Keep still. I've got to dig deeper.

PATIENT

Ow, ow! That hurt. Have you got it?

DOCTOR

No. That was a lump of wax and a ball of cotton wool.

PATIENT

I can't stand much more of this. Hurry up.

DOCTOR

It's nearly over now.

PATIENT

Have you got him? I can't bear it any more.

Sound PAGE 11

DOCTOR

Keep still, I don't want to hurt the poor little fellow. Here he comes now. Got him.

PATIENT

You mean he's out?

DOCTOR

Yes. Just look at him. **(Doctor studies the earwig closely)**

PATIENT

No more pain. I'll never go camping again.

DOCTOR

Oh dear. I think you'd better come back next week.

PATIENT

Why? What for?

DOCTOR

I'm afraid it isn't a little fellow after all. It's a little lady. And I'm afraid she's just laid her eggs. In your ear.

Sound PAGE 12

PATIENT

Oh no!

Exit Doctor and Patient

Adapted from "AN EARWIG IN THE EAR" by Nigel Gray

Four children enter. Three of them are carrying a model or a large drawing of the ear which can be referred to as they speak. The following section has been written by children as a result of their own research and is given as an example. Children may write and read their own research

FIRST CHILD

The ear is an amazing and complex part of the body. The bit that sticks out of your head, the outer ear, is only part of the ear. The rest of the ear is inside your head.

SECOND CHILD

The outer ear is shaped like a funnel to collect sounds and direct them inside your head. The sounds, in the form of vibrating air, hit a thin sheet of skin called the eardrum and make it shake.

THIRD CHILD

The middle ear contains three tiny bones, the hammer, the anvil and the stirrup. These increase the vibrations from the eardrum and pass them on to the inner ear.

Sound

FOURTH CHILD

In the inner ear, a shell shaped organ, called the cochlea, changes the vibrations into electrical messages. These messages are carried to the brain along nerves. The brain interprets the messages it receives and we hear the sound.

NARRATOR

When the ears do not function properly, the result is partial or total deafness. A cold, the change in air pressure in an aircraft when flying or very loud disco music can cause temporary deafness. Problems with the bones in the middle ear can sometimes be helped with a hearing aid. Damaged sound nerves in the inner ear result in no signals being sent to the brain and, therefore, total deafness.

PRAYER

We thank You God for the endless variety of sounds,
For the song of the birds, the patter of raindrops,
The whistling wind and the rustling of leaves.
Give us sympathy for those who cannot hear and live in a silent world.

AMEN

Children sing

"SOUNDS OF SILENCE" as sung by Simon & Garfunkel.

Notes

Music

PAGE 1

ATTAINMENT TARGETS
SCIENCE: AT14 Sound and Music: Levels 1, 2b, 3a, 5a.
ENGLISH: AT1 Speaking and Listening: Levels 1, 2a, 2d, 2e, 4, 5d, 6b, 6c.
AT2 Reading: Levels 3a, 4a.
TECHNOLOGY: AT1 Identifying needs and opportunities: Levels 2c, 3b, 4a, 5a, 6c.
AT2 Generating a design: Levels 1, 2a, 3, 4, 5a, 5b, 5c, 5d, 6a, 6c.
AT3 Planning and making: Levels 2a, 2b, 2c, 3, 4b, 4c, 4d, 4e, 5.
AT4 Evaluating: Levels 2a, 3a, 3b, 4a, 4b, 5a, 5b.

CHARACTERS

Up to 10 Narrators
Children with musical instruments
Children with instruments they have made
Mayor
Pied Piper
Rats
Children
Members of Hamelin Council
6 Minstrels
Handel
Bach
Beethoven
Mendelssohn
Shirley Temple
Elvis Presley
Chorus
Prayer Leader

NARRATOR

The story of music goes back to the first people who lived on Earth. Their music was very different from music as we know it today. Loud noises could be made by banging stones and sticks together and they found that they could make whistling sounds by blowing through pieces of reindeer horn, reeds and shells. People first made music for magical or religious reasons and so music has played an important part in religion ever since. The music that they made was also useful for frightening off wild animals and for expressing their feelings, whether happy or sad.

Music

PAGE 2

All children sing

"MUSIC WAS MY FIRST LOVE" by John Miles

NARRATOR

All the sounds that we hear are caused by some kind of vibration. All musical instruments have a part which vibrates and a hollow sound box which makes the sound louder. To produce a musical sound you have to set something vibrating. There are five main groups of musical instrument; stringed, woodwind, brass, percussion and keyboard.

**As each group of musical instruments is introduced, a child enters carrying at least one instrument from each group.
The children can play their instruments to demonstrate different musical sounds**

All children sing

"I AM THE MUSIC MAN" Playgroup Favourites – EMI (Cassette)

As the children sing about the instruments above, the child holding the instrument they are singing about, will act as if playing it

NARRATOR

Making your own musical instruments is not a very difficult task and you do not need expensive tools or materials.

Children enter with a range of musical instruments which they have made themselves. They can explain how each instrument was made and perhaps perform as a "skiffle" group

Music — PAGE 3

NARRATOR

In Old Testament times, when the Jews settled in the Promised Land of Palestine, their musical instruments included a drum, rather like a tambourine, a lyre or small harp and a flute. These were the instruments of the wandering tribesmen, simple to make and simple to play. They also used a ram's horn and a loud metal trumpet for fanfares.

In Africa, traditional instruments are still made from materials which can be found around the village. Drums are made from hollowed logs and animal skins. Every important occasion such as the birth of a baby or a marriage has special music and dancing to go with it.

NARRATOR

Music is all around us. Different kinds of music can affect us in different ways. Loud, noisy music can make us feel excited. Quiet, gentle music helps us to relax. Some music makes us feel happy and other music can make us feel sad. Music seems to have almost magical powers in that it can change the way we are feeling. The rats and the children in Robert Browning's story of The Pied Piper of Hamelin, were so fascinated by the sweet, soft notes played by the piper that they forgot about everything else.

Music — PAGE 4

NARRATOR

The town of Hamelin was overrun with rats. The people became very angry and demanded that the Mayor and the council find some means of ridding the town of the rats immediately.

Enter Mayor and councillors

MAYOR

Oh for a trap, a trap, a trap!

NARRATOR

Just as he said this, what should hap
At the chamber door but a gentle tap?

MAYOR

Come in!

NARRATOR

The Mayor cried, looking bigger:
And in did come the strangest figure!
(Enter Pied Piper)
He advanced to the council-table:

PIED PIPER

Please your honours, I'm able,
By means of a secret charm, to draw
All creatures living beneath the sun,
That creep or swim or fly or run,
After me so as you never saw!
And I chiefly use my charm
On creatures that cause people alarm,
The mole and toad and newt and viper;
And people call me the Pied Piper.
If I can rid your town of rats
Will you give me a thousand guilders?

MAYOR

One thousand? We'll give you fifty thousand guilders!

NARRATOR

Was the exclamation
Of the astonished Mayor and Corporation.
Into the streets the Piper stepped,
Smiling first a little smile,
As if he knew what magic slept
In his quiet pipe the while;
Then, like a musical adept,
To blow the pipe his lips he wrinkled,
And green and blue his sharp eyes twinkled,
Like a candle-flame where salt is sprinkled;
And ere three shrill notes the pipe uttered,
You heard as though an army muttered;

continued . . .

And the muttering grew to a grumbling;
And the grumbling grew to a mighty rumbling;
And out of the houses the rats came tumbling.
(Enter rats)
Brother, sisters, husbands, wives–
Followed the Piper for their lives.
From street to street he piped advancing,
And step for step they followed dancing,
Until they came to the river Weser
Wherein all plunged and perished!

All exit

NARRATOR

Suddenly, up the face
Of the Piper perked in the market-place,

(Enter Pied Piper, Mayor and Council)

PIED PIPER

First, if you please, my thousand guilders!

MAYOR

A thousand guilders! Come, we'll only give you one hundred!

PIPED PIPER

Folks who put me in a passion
May find me pipe in another fashion.

Music — PAGE 7

MAYOR

You threaten us, fellow? Do your worst,
Blow your pipe there till you burst!

NARRATOR

Once more he stepped into the street.
And to his lips again
Laid his long pipe of smooth straight cane;
And ere he blew three notes (such sweet soft notes)
There was a rustling, that seemed like a bustling
Of merry crowds jostling and pitching and hustling,
(Enter children)
Small feet were pattering, wooden shoes clattering,
Little hands clapping and little tongues chattering,
And, like fowls in a farmyard when barley is scattering,
Out came the children running.
All the little boys and girls,
With rosy cheeks and flaxen curls,
And sparkling eyes and teeth like pearls,
Tripping and skipping, ran merrily after
The wonderful music with shouting and laughter.

The mayor was dumb, and the Council stood
As if they were changed into blocks of wood,
Unable to move a step, or cry
To the children merrily skipping by.
– Could only follow with the eye
That joyous crowd at the Piper's back.
But how the mayor was on the rack,
And the wretched Council's bosoms beat,
As the Piper turned from the High Street

Music — PAGE 8

To where the Weser rolled its waters
Right in the way of their sons and daughters!
However he turned from South to West,
And to Koppelberg Hill his steps addressed,
And after him the children pressed;
Great was the joy in every breast.

When, lo, as they reached the mountain-side,
A wondrous portal opened wide,
As if a cavern was suddenly hollowed;
And the Piper advanced and the children followed.
And when all were in to the very last,
The door in the mountain-side shut fast.

All exit

NARRATOR

Music is an unsolved mystery. We still don't really know why we respond to music in the way we do. People in ancient times considered music to be a gift from the gods. Men thought that the world was full of demons and spirits. It was important to please the spirits and to keep them happy – and music and dancing were a way of doing this. Most religions, throughout the world, still make use of music, from chanting in Buddhist temples to hymns in the Christian church. Music helps worshippers to join in the service because they can sing psalms, anthems and hymns.

Suggested hymns: "LET ALL THE WORLD IN EVERY CORNER SING" (TTS)
"GIVE ME JOY IN MY HEART" (MHB)

Music

PAGE 9

NARRATOR

Everyone in the human race can sing. It is as though we have two voices. One is for talking and reading and one is for singing. You can say a sentence or you can sing it. To sing the words you seem to have to lift up your voice. When we talk about high notes and low notes in music, we use the word "pitch". A high pitch is produced by faster or more frequent vibrations, and a lower pitch by slower vibrations. The number of vibrations per second is called a note's frequency. Pitches are just like steps on a ladder. Each step is a different pitch. When notes go up or down, one step at a time, they play a "scale".

All pupils sing

"DO – RE – MI" from "The Sound of Music"
written by **Rodgers & Hammerstein**

NARRATOR

Singing, like the first musical instruments, probably began with early man. He uttered cries and stamped his feet to produce rhythms. The Book of Psalms in the Old Testament is the oldest song book still in use. The 23rd Psalm is one of the most famous.

Suggested Hymn: "THE LORD'S MY SHEPHERD"
by **W. Whittingham and F. Rous (MHB)**

NARRATOR

Over the centuries there have been many famous composers of music. We would like to introduce you to some of them.

Music

PAGE 10

Enter a group of 6 minstrels

1ST MINSTREL

I am proud to present to you, "The Gleemen", a troupe of wandering minstrels who will entertain you in their own special way. We play music and we sing songs, we juggle and we perform acrobatics.
(The minstrels perform)

Minstrels sing

"A WANDERING MINSTREL I" from "THE MIKADO"
by **Gilbert and Sullivan.**

Enter Handel to excerpt from "THE MESSIAH"

HANDEL

My name is George Frideric Handel. I was born in Germany in 1685. I have written 50 operas and 20 oratorios. An oratorio is a religious opera which tells a Bible story. My most famous oratorio is the music you are listening to. It is called "The Messiah".

Enter Bach to excerpt from "JESU, JOY OF MAN'S DESIRING"

BACH

My name is Johann Sebastian Bach. I was born in Germany in 1685. I began my musical life as a choir boy, singing and learning the violin, harpsichord and organ. I became a famous organist but I am best known for composing music for instruments and church music like the piece you are listening to, which is called "Jesu, Joy of Man's Desiring".

Music — PAGE 11

Enter Beethoven to excerpt from "SYMPHONY NO. 9, THE CHORAL"

BEETHOVEN

My name is Ludwig van Beethoven. I was born in Germany in 1770. In my late twenties, I began to lose my hearing and eventually became completely deaf. Despite this, I continued to write music including the piece you are listening to now, "The Choral Symphony".

Enter Mendelssohn to excerpt from "THE HEBRIDES OVERTURE, FINGAL'S CAVE"

MENDELSSOHN

My name is Felix Mendelssohn. I was born in Germany in 1809. I had written 15 symphonies and an opera before I was 15 years old. In 1842, I visited Britain and played the piano for Queen Victoria and Prince Albert. When I visited Scotland, the scenery inspired me to write the music you are listening to. It is called "Fingal's Cave".

NARRATOR

Popular music has always existed alongside the more serious classical music and has come to be known as "pop". At the beginning of the twentieth century, Music Halls were built and the songs sung here were the big hits of the time.

All children sing

"DOWN AT THE OLD BULL AND BUSH" (GBSB)

Music — PAGE 12

NARRATOR

During the First World War when British troops were marching off to the horrors of the trenches, songs were written to cheerful tunes to try and raise their spirits.

All children sing

"IT"S A LONG WAY TO TIPPERARY" (TA)

NARRATOR

In 1927 when a singer called Al Jolson said, "You ain't heard nothing yet folks!" he really meant it. The invention of film soundtrack meant that the audience heard just as much music as talk. Shirley Temple, at the age of seven, became the world's number one box-office attraction, singing;

Enter Shirley Temple who sings

"ON THE GOOD SHIP LOLLIPOP"

NARRATOR

In the 1950s, rock n' roll became very popular with young people all over America and later in Europe. Elvis Presley was the most successful rock n' roll singer.

Enter rock n' roll dancers and Elvis Presley who sings

"JAILHOUSE ROCK"

Music

PAGE 13

NARRATOR

In the early 1960s pop music in England began to be played by "groups". The Beatles were the first group to become world-famous.

All children sing

"YELLOW SUBMARINE"

NARRATOR

The worldwide spread of music in the 20th century means that we can now hear all kinds of different sounds such as Indian sitars and finger-cymbals. Electronic equipment like synthesizers and computers are used side by side with older instruments. No sound seems impossible. What the music of the next century will be like no one knows. What is important is that we never stop listening to and making music. Music is a gift which can give immense enjoyment and pleasure to all.

PRAYER

Dear God,
Through all the lovely sounds we hear
Help us to feel You very near. . .
Dear God,
To whom we all belong,
Thank You for Music and for Song.

All children sing

"THANK YOU FOR THE MUSIC" as sung by Abba.

Notes

Notes

Notes

Notes

Notes

Notes

Notes